PYRAMIDS

SMITHSONIAN
EXPLORING THE ANCIENT WORLD
JEREMY A. SABLOFF, Editor

PYRAMIDS

By FLORA SIMMONS CLANCY

St. Remy Press • Montreal

Smithsonian Books • Washington, D.C.

EXPLORING THE ANCIENT WORLD
was produced by
ST. REMY PRESS

Publisher	Kenneth Winchester
President	Pierre Léveillé
Managing Editor	Carolyn Jackson
Managing Art Director	Diane Denoncourt
Production Manager	Michelle Turbide
Administrator	Natalie Watanabe

Staff for *PYRAMIDS*

Editors	Michael Ballantyne
	Alfred LeMaitre
Art Director	Philippe Arnoldi
Picture Editor	Christopher Jackson
Researcher	Olga Dzatko
Assistant Editor	Jennifer Meltzer
Photo Assistant	Geneviève Monette
Photo Researcher	Neale McDevitt
Illustrator	Maryo Proulx
Systems Coordinator	Jean-Luc Roy
Administrative Assistant	Dominique Gagné
Indexer	Christine Jacobs
Proofreader	Judy Yelon

THE SMITHSONIAN INSTITUTION

Secretary	Robert McC. Adams
Assistant Secretary for External Affairs	Thomas E. Lovejoy
Director, Smithsonian Institution Press	Felix C. Lowe

SMITHSONIAN BOOKS

Editor-in-Chief	Patricia Gallagher
Senior Editor	Alexis Doster III
Editors	Amy Donovan
	Joe Goodwin
Assistant Editors	Brian D. Kennedy
	Sonia Reece
Senior Picture Editor	Frances C. Rowsell
Picture Editors	Carrie F. Bruns
	R. Jenny Takacs
Picture Research	V. Susan Guardado
Production Editor	Patricia Upchurch
Business Manager	Stephen J. Bergstrom

Library of Congress Cataloging-in-Publication Data
Clancy, Flora S.
    Pyramids / Flora S. Clancy
        p. cm. — (Exploring the ancient world)
    Includes bibliographical references and index.
    ISBN 0-89599-039-3
    1. Indians of Mexico—Pyramids. 2. Pyramids—Cross-cultural studies. 3. Pyramids—Latin America 4. Latin America—Antiquities. I. Title. II. Series.
    F1219.3.P9C53   1994
    972—dc20   94-18949
                                                    CIP

Manufactured and printed in Canada.
First Edition

10 9 8 7 6 5 4 3 2 1

FRONT COVER PHOTO: *The pyramids of the Giza plateau, outside modern-day Cairo, define the Western conception of the pyramid as a memorial to a departed ruler.*

BACK COVER PHOTO: *The sculptured image of the Cakravartin, or Buddhist god-king, recurs constantly on the temple-towers of Angkor Wat, Cambodia.*

CONTENTS

EDITOR'S FOREWORD

Pyramid is one of those magical words that immediately conjures up strong visual images whenever one sees or hears it. More often than not, the image that comes to mind is that of the great Egyptian pyramids at Giza, outside of modern-day Cairo. These pyramids, as well as others throughout the ancient world, have been the subject of a tremendous number of commentaries. Some of these are reasonable, but many—unfortunately—are not!

Professor Flora Clancy's book falls well into the former camp and provides a challenging, intellectually stimulating overview of pyramid traditions throughout the preindustrial world. Her discussion combines clear understandings of the available archaeological, art historical, and architectural data on pyramid-building, as well as a lucid grasp of ancient religions. She offers some dazzling insights into the functions and meanings of pyramids, and corrects many myths and biases about these structures. Among these are the argument that "better" pyramids were ones that were built to last for millennia, or the misconception that the Roman arch is a superior architectural form to the corbel vault.

Using a broad definition of pyramids, which encompasses Mesopotamian ziggurats, Buddhist stupas, Khmer temple-towers, and Maya terraced pyramids among others, Professor Clancy makes breathtaking comparisons of widespread similarities and differences in pyramid traditions. Within the context of her wide cross-cultural comparison, she is able, for example, to demonstrate convincingly that the Egyptian pyramids are not the exemplars of worldwide pyramid building, but rather the exception.

In her wide-ranging treatment of ancient pyramids, Professor Clancy addresses many of the questions that interested laypeople frequently ask about these monumental constructions, including "how were they built?" She describes the various construction techniques and clearly demonstrates that the construction of pyramids, whether in Egypt or in Mexico, was eminently feasible on both technical and mechanical grounds. She convincingly shows that preindustrial peoples in the Old and New Worlds were quite capable of erecting these monuments, and possessed both the engineering and planning capabilities required, as well as the capacity to quarry and transport building materials, as well as the physical labor to undertake the actual building. There is no need to invoke (or any evidence to support) claims that pyramids were constructed with the help of aliens or superhumans.

Professor Clancy also considers the questions "why were the pyramids built?" and "what were their functions?" In answering such questions, she discusses the ideological, political, and economic implications of pyramid construction. She shows how pyramids were often viewed by ancient peoples as metaphorical mountains that linked the material world with both heaven and the underworld. She also analyzes the frequent associations of pyramids with caves and with water. In addition, she provides fascinating hypotheses about why such "unnecessary projects" as the construction of pyramids were undertaken across vast stretches of space and time.

Professor Clancy concludes her examination of pyramids by classifying them into two major traditions. The first includes pyramids that served principally as memorials, while the second includes those that functioned as stages for dramatic events. She carefully dissects these two traditions and indicates the significant implications of their differences and similarities.

Professor Clancy received her doctorate from Yale University and currently is Professor of Art History at the University of New Mexico. She is well known and respected for her productive merging of both art historical and archaeological approaches to the monumental art and architecture of ancient Mesoamerica. Dr. Clancy is the co-editor of *Vision and Revision in Maya Studies* (1990) and a major contributor to *Maya: Treasures of an Ancient Civilization* (1985). She also has a number of other scholarly publications to her credit.

No matter how familiar readers think they are with the pyramids of Africa, the Near East, Asia, and the Americas, I am certain they will find many new ideas and much food for thought in the pages that follow. I invite you to join Professor Clancy in her intellectual voyage to the pyramids of the ancient world.

Jeremy A. Sabloff
University of Pennsylvania Museum of
Archaeology and Anthropology

PREFACE

Pyramids are forms of logic. They represent compellingly convincing forces in our histories: literally, as an architecture with undeniable structural integrity, and metaphorically, as visible and monumental expressions of human thought. This statement was not my original premise; rather, it emerged from the writing of the book. The original premise had to do with displacing the famed Egyptian pyramid as the paradigm for all pyramids, by showing how unusual the structure is when compared to other types of pyramids, and with a desire to explore ideological points of view in order to balance certain materialistic and spiritualistic explanations for the presence of pyramids in our histories. There was also, at the start of this project, a vague sense that all pyramids represented the human hope for a greater reality than our existential one, and that a sensible connection to our cosmos and our gods was possible. These original premises have not been entirely erased from the following chapters, because it is through them that a different perception, and a number of questions, were formed: pyramids are different, but just how are they different, and why?

This book begins with an examination of how points of view influence, and have influenced, our view of pyramids. Then follows a fairly lengthy chapter describing the pyramids built by various peoples throughout the world: in the Americas, in the Near East and Africa, in India and Southeast Asia, and in China. It is not an inclusive survey but, nonetheless, a general one; one that frankly has had to rely on available literature and whether any extensive archaeological work had been done and published. Some may feel that undue emphasis has been placed on the pyramids of ancient Mesoamerica, but this is my area of scholarly expertise and represents the basis for my point of view throughout the book.

Chapter 3 presents the ways in which pyramids are constructed by focusing on the architectural aspects of plan, internal massing, elevation, and external embellishments. The economics of building a pyramid are also discussed because construction techniques and the economic means of building a pyramid must be sensitive to laws that are constant and not subject to historical or cultural desires. The laws of gravity are the same the world over, and building a monument requires a lot of energy.

The functions and ideologies of pyramids are the topics of Chapter 4 and

The best known pyramid shape is the geometric or battered profile, with its square base and triangular sides, of which the Great Pyramid of Khufu (Cheops) at Giza, in Egypt, is the most famous example. Often thought of as the paradigm for all pyramids, the Great Pyramid's geometric shape remains more firmly etched in our minds than the more common stepped form.

are elicited from the descriptions of the two previous chapters. That is, function and ideology are related to, and come out of, the particulars of history and form. While critical (but not always in the carping sense of critique) of previous and current interpretations of function and the roles of ideology, Chapter 4 builds to Chapter 5 wherein a direct relationship is drawn between the history, construction, and shape of a pyramid, and its functional and ideological meanings. The two basic shapes in the history of pyramids, the geometric shape and the stepped shape, are characterized as memorials and stages, respectively. The geometric shapes are closed to human participation after their initial completion, while the stepped shapes were built for continuing human interaction, because their stages were made accessible by stairways, and because they supported temples for continuing ritual and ceremony. The closed pyramid is characterized as representing beliefs for a pre-existent and revealed reality about the human condition, while the open pyramid represents beliefs in a reality that is still negotiable.

Captured in this watercolor by British artist David Roberts, the Great Sphinx guards the mighty pyramids at Giza. Following Napoleon's campaign reports of the massive monuments along the Nile. Paintings like this one were a source of great interest to a public clamoring for more information

PYRAMIDS AND POINTS OF VIEW

Agreat many books have been written about pyramids—so many, in fact, that if all the pages of all the books, notes, and letters discussing pyramids were laid down together, they would probably equal, and perhaps even surpass, the mass of the Great Pyramid of Egypt. For the historian, this body of literature is noteworthy in itself, regardless of the information it contains. It represents tangible evidence of the remarkable variety of ways—historical, archaeological, and ideological—in which pyramids

in Egypt, the Western world became enthralled by
on these fascinating structures.

have been, and continue to be, looked at and thought about. It represents a manifest profundity behind our fascination for ancient and majestic monuments.

ARCHAEOLOGICAL AND HISTORICAL POINTS OF VIEW

Almost no story of the Egyptian pyramids, at least no archaeological or historical view, begins without a discussion of the *History,* by the Greek historian and geographer Herodotus, written sometime in the middle of the fifth century B.C. Herodotus visited the ancient Egyptian pyramids on the Giza plateau. In discussing the Great Pyramid of Khufu (or Cheops), he gives a lot of factual information, or perhaps one should say, pragmatic information, because Herodotus is often accused of starting, or at least perpetuating, "innumerable inaccuracies concerning the pyramids," according to author Desmond Steward. Still, it is wonderful to read that it took 1600 talents of silver to pay for all the radishes, onions, and garlic consumed by the laborers working on the Great Pyramid. (The perceived inaccuracies may originate more from subsequent translations and interpretations than from Herodotus's failings as a reliable observer.)

The British scholar Leonard Cottrell has produced a philological history of the many authors and scholars who have written about the Egyptian pyramids. The reader who wishes a closer look at these commentators—ranging from the biblical Jeremiah; the remarkably lucid descriptions of the Arab historian Abd-el-Latif, written in the 12th century; the calculations of the Scottish pyramid-mystic Charles Piazzi Smyth; to the eminent British scientist-archaeologist, Flinders Petrie—can find such information in Cottrell's fine and readable, but now dated, text.

As described in the introduction to Gordon R. Willey and Jeremy A. Sabloff's seminal book, *A History of American Archaeology,* the goals of the historian and the archaeologist are really the same: "*to narrate* the sequent story of [the] past and *to explain* the events that composed it." Archaeology is a scientific discipline, and history belongs to the humanities. That the historian and the archaeologist offer different narrations with differing explanations has to do with the primary data they use. The archaeologist will narrate the story of the pyramid by using the "hard" data of material forms and objects procured from excavation and survey. The historian draws his or her story from the "soft" data of ancient texts, travelers' descriptions, and other historians' work.

In an interesting reversal, the historian may use soft data, but seeks to define real, or what could be described as "hard" times, and the archaeologist using hard data will tell his or her story in soft time. This needs explaining. The soft data of the historian who is looking at ancient texts comes from the fact that any written text, modern or ancient, must be interpreted and that interpretations by different historians looking at the same text can vary, sometimes widely, often giving rise to remarkably heated arguments. The current, and heated, debates over the interpretation of the Dead Sea Scrolls are a good example.

Fifth-century-B.C. Greek historian and geographer Herodotus traveled extensively in the ancient world, and visited the pyramids on the Giza plateau. He is credited as one of the originators of Western written history.

Excavations of the Pyramid of the Magician, at Uxmal, in the Yucatán, Mexico, have helped establish that it was built during five construction periods spanning several centuries. It contains evidence of four separate temples that were subsequently buried when the fifth and final one was built. The quality of the cut stone of this and other Maya structures impressed those who worked on its restoration.

The data to be found in ancient texts is equivocal—soft time. Nonetheless, the task of the historian who studies the pyramids is to find out, if possible, who built them and when, that is, actual names and dates. Cautiously, the historian will write "circa" before an uncertain date, but the effort will continue in the hopes of finding the document that clears the date of its prefix—hard time.

Archaeologists work with unequivocal, material data: their tunnels dug into the ancient Pyramid of the Magician at Uxmal, in the Yucatán, Mexico, reveal smaller structures within it, whose facing stones and plan-outlines can be traced. Clearly, the inner buildings were built before the outer, visible one. Through comparisons—between the kinds of construction fills used in one building to another, or between different buildings—a more refined statement about the durations between structures can be made, perhaps refined even more through the modern techniques of radiocarbon dating. Even so, the archaeologist is paying attention to relative dates expressing durations of time—relative or soft time.

Well into the 19th century, however, what we separate into the distinct disciplines of history and archaeology was subsumed by the term and role of the antiquarian whose work consisted of description, deductive and inductive arguments, and critical assessments of the works of previous commentators. Many expeditions were undertaken at this time, funded by countries—especially France and England—mandating the "discovery" and "excavation" of royal tombs and the bringing back of treasures to grace private collections and the newly popular national museums. With the deciphering of Egyptian hieroglyphs by the French scholar Jean-François Champollion in the early 19th century, the primary texts written by the ancient Egyptians themselves became available to historical scrutiny, and greater certainty was achieved for historical concerns with names and dates. And in the middle of the 19th century, archaeologists became more rigorous in their excavations by turning their attention to the whole array of material remains—not just treasures—and establishing scientific, testable, and repeatable methods for assessing these artifacts. Chief among their methodologies was the use of stratigraphy for relative dating and seriation typologies for establishing types or families of related artifacts.

The early 19th-century French scholar Jean-François Champollion was enthralled by Egypt and its history. At a very young age, he mastered the Coptic language. The Rosetta Stone (*right*), a block of basalt inscribed in three scripts and two languages, was discovered in 1799 by French soldiers in Egypt. The decipherment and translation of its hieroglyphic, demotic, and Greek text posed a challenge to many scholarly minds. It was Champollion who eventually unlocked the linguistic key, and thus led the way to the decipherment of texts from the vanished civilization of ancient Egypt.

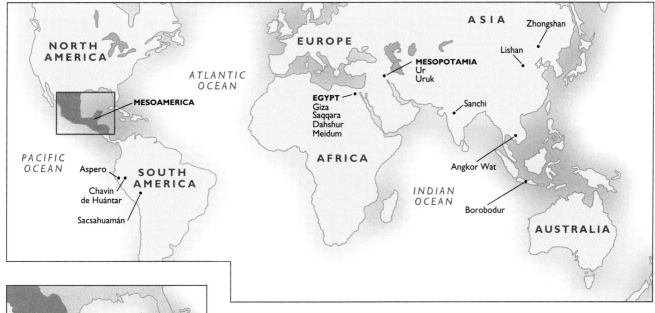

MESOAMERICA

Pyramids have been built at different times by peoples all over the world, and their locations range from the coastal deserts of Peru to the jungles of Java. For the most part, the world's pyramid-building traditions are not connected historically, but archaeologists continue to make comparisons between forms and building techniques of pyramids and the traditions from which they arose in order to better understand both the structures themselves and the cultures that produced them.

Although our modern stories and explanations are different than those of the 19th century, today there is often little that distinguishes the writings of the historian from those of the archaeologist, and often the disciplines are practiced by the same person. *The Pyramids of Egypt* by I.E.S. Edwards is a comprehensive history written by a well-known archaeologist versed in the historical learning of hieroglyphs, ancient myths, names, and dates. The art historian Heinrich Zimmer's great work, *The Art of Indian Asia*, displays his full control over the archaeological facts available to him. What seems to be the case is that historians and archaeologists happily use the "hard data" achieved by the other, while reinterpreting or rejecting each other's "soft data."

However, another disciplinary distinction remains, and it is important. As Willey and Sabloff point out in the introduction to their book, an important method in the work of both historians and archaeologists is the drawing of comparisons to order and elucidate their material. The historian draws on comparisons that are within, or can be shown to be historically connected to, the period or history that is being studied. It does no good to study ancient Maya hieroglyphs carved within the temples atop pyramids raised in the Guatemalan jungles to further the known history of Egyptian pyramids. Archaeologists, on the other hand, can and do make comparisons between the forms and building techniques of widely different traditions, such as ancient Maya pyramidal forms compared with Khmer temple-towers. They make no claims for historical connections, but try to elucidate through abstract comparisons possible similarities and differences in forms that lead to a better understanding of function, and of the cultures that conceived the forms. Historians' comparisons will be restricted by time, person, and place (their hard data), while those of archaeologists will be limited to forms and patterns (their hard data).

In the Near East and Africa, there is a kind of equality in the data available to the historian and the archaeologist; other areas of the world are not as lucidly depicted by history, because few or no contemporary writings survive to be deciphered and interpreted. Until recently, the historian of ancient Mesoamerica, for example, had nothing else to work with except the hard data of the archaeologist. The historian could, and usually did, change the archaeologist's story to arrive at a different explanation, but this would be done through deductive reasoning.

When the ancient site of Tula, located north of Mexico City, was first excavated in the 1930s, its formal, architectural comparisons to the contemporary (10th-13th century) Maya site of Chichén Itzá (in the Yucatán) were quickly realized by archaeologists. The explanatory story or narrative is: Toltec Tula was the origin and source of what was seen as a Mexican or Toltec influence in the Maya region. Through conquest and trade, the Toltecs became the rulers of Chichén Itzá and were the major patrons of the last architectural projects, of which the Temple of the Warriors was understood as an almost direct copy of Structure B from the home site of Tula.

To many scholars, the design of the Maya Temple of the Warriors, at Chichén Itzá, Mexico, appeared to be greatly influenced by Structure B at the Toltec site of Tula. A more recent interpretation of the relationship between the two cultures challenges this view. It points out that Chichén Itzá was a more highly developed center, built on a grander scale, implying that the architectural influence might have originated with the Maya.

In the 1960s, the art historian George Kubler challenged and reversed this interpretation, pointing out that the city of Chichén Itzá was much grander in size and its architecture more fully developed in form and style than anything found at Tula. By deduction, Kubler suggested that, if there was influential communication between the two sites—and surely there was—its direction must have been from the more developed style of Chichén Itzá's architectural forms to the comparatively provincial style of Tula. Colonial chronicles written in both the Mexican and the Mayan regions during the 16th and 17th centuries tell of Toltec-Mexican presence in the Yucatán but mainly through a story about the journey of the mythic hero, Quetzalcóatl, from Tula to the Yucatán. While one can easily read politics and conquest into these stories, as with most texts, they are debatable and equivocal and can be interpreted to favor both explanations.

SPIRITUAL POINTS OF VIEW

There is in all writings about pyramids, whether anecdotal or scholarly, a sense of wonder about the pyramid itself and an underlying conviction about its

The Pyramid of Tlahuizcalpantecuhtli (known more prosaically as Structure B) in Tula, Mexico, is a carefully restored Toltec structure from circa A.D. 1000 that shows clear and uncomplicated symmetry in its horizontal tiers.

encapsulation of the knowledge and wisdom of its builders. Taken literally, the events of discovery and revelation are the pillars on which a large body of pyramid literature rests. Leonard Cottrell coined the term "pyramidiot" to characterize the pyramidologist and his or her belief in the Egyptian pyramids as perfect expressions of ancient and eternal wisdom, awaiting only our abilities to uncover or decipher these expressions to discover their "secrets." For the most part, these kinds of efforts have focused on the Egyptian pyramids, but more recently, Mesoamerican pyramids have also been studied for their wisdom, usually thought to be embedded in numerology and mathematics.

Because of his passionate and engaging prose, Charles Piazzi Smyth, Astronomer Royal of Scotland, is the most famous 19th-century pyramidologist. He was not the first student of pyramid mysteries; there is a long history. Cottrell suggests that Arab commentators in the ninth century were the first to discuss the mystical (not just mythical) qualities supposedly embedded in the pyramids. Piazzi Smyth, drawing heavily on an older colleague—John Taylor, author of the 1859 work *The Great Pyramid: Why Was It Built and Who Built*

It?—put forward the thesis that the Great Pyramid was not a tomb but a monumental repository for an inspired system of measurements, volumes and weights based on universal principles, such as recording the values of pi, a ratio supposedly unknown to the ancients. The whole display of his painstaking efforts at measuring the Great Pyramid at Giza, its gallery, passages, and its "coffer" (Smyth considered coffin the wrong label for the stone sarcophagus found in the King's Chamber) is astounding, but when he went on to demonstrate that the pyramid embeds human history and, more specifically, Christian history in its measurements, he lit a torch for all future pyramidiots.

Working a century later, Peter Lemesurier and Peter Tompkins, both publishing in the 1970s, draw from the newly established field of archaeoastronomy to bolster and enlarge the main theses of Taylor and Smyth. Lemesurier argues that the message of the Great Pyramid is given as a code, "in terms of mathematics—which is the only truly universal language," to relate a "record of all that was past and of all things to come." He considers the Great Pyramid's descending passage's angle of incline, which scholars have shown to point to the north node, as pointing to Bethlehem and, by virtue of this, a prophecy of the birth of Jesus Christ. Remarkably, he goes on to explain that this prophecy is better understood through a "cyclic view of history" as something always happening, and here he draws upon the *Chilam Balam of the Chumayel*, a compendium of history and prophecy written in Yucatecan Maya between the 18th century and the present.

After publishing *Secrets of the Great Pyramid* in 1971, Peter Tompkins brought out *Mysteries of the Mexican Pyramids* in 1976. In it, he illustrates the drawings and calculations by Hugh Harleston, Jr., which show how, because of its measurements and ratios, the Pyramid of the Sun at Teotihuacán fully participates in the same mysteries discovered within the Egyptian pyramid, as an architectural "diagram," or manifestation of the Planet Earth within its solar system.

H. Spencer Lewis, the famous Rosicrucian—a member of a society professing esoteric religious principles—is perhaps the most engaging of the 20th-century pyramidologists. In the introduction to his 1936 book, *The Symbolic Prophecy of the Great Pyramid*, he flatly states that his book is "the presentation of the mystical side of the pyramid...." The reader is not beleaguered with pages of quasi-scientific lists of measurements and ratios, but is treated to a straightforward account of how the pyramid was built for mystical ceremonies of initiation and "coincidentally, as a monument for the preservation of wisdom [and prophecy]."

The roots of the pyramidologist or pyramidiot probably go back to the time the pyramids were built, but their flowering arrived with the antiquarians of the 19th century. The continuation of such anecdotal descriptions and mystical interpretations into the 20th century can be understood as a romantic rebellion against the onslaughts of the objective sciences, but just as surely, it reverberates with the very human hope for order and cosmic justification mentioned in the preface.

The interior of the Great
Pyramid of Giza contains
a complicated network of
passages designed to deter
intruders from reaching the
sacred tomb of the Great
Pharaoh Khufu (Cheops).
This 19th-century engraving
by Luigi Mayer depicts the
problems faced by those
ascending the steep and
narrow passage between the
second and third galleries.

The pyramids of Egypt were carefully laid out along the cardinal directions, possibly emphasizing the theory of the time that the world of humankind could be positively aligned to the larger universe.

IDEOLOGICAL POINTS OF VIEW

Both archaeologists and historians—and pyramidiots, for that matter—express ideas in their narrations for, and explanations of, the pyramids. Ideas are ephemeral but they leave material traces, and the attempt to understand the ideologies embedded in archaeological and historical remains is often like solving a mystery. However, there are always at least two ideologies present in the works by scholars and writers: the scholar's personal ideologies along with his or her perceived ideologies for the historic or prehistoric peoples being scrutinized. Archaeologists and anthropologists use the terms "etic" and "emic" to distinguish between these ideological sets. They are not terms generally used by or applied to historians, but obviously the distinction would hold for them as well.

An emic point of view is generated from within the things or events studied, and is characterized as subjective, while an etic point of view is generated from without, and is considered objective. For example, suppose two anthropologists are studying a people who still hunt for their food. One anthropologist does so by living with the people, learning their skills, and joining them on their hunts. In his published reports, he tries to relate how the hunters saw their world, how they talked about it, and how they explained it. Ideally, he tries not to impose his own ideas about reality in an effort to allow an unbiased representation of the hunter's own, or emic, point of view. The other anthropologist, maintaining an etic point of view, goes into the field with the questions he is going to ask already prepared. He does not know the answers to his questions, but his questions purposively structure the kinds of things to be elicited. In other words, he has a problem he wishes to solve, but his concerns may be of little interest to the people he is studying. The report of the emic point of view reads like a diary, a narrative based largely on tape-recorded transcriptions. The report of the etic point of view is analytical, with comparative illustrations to show how the particulars of these hunters fit into the larger realities of a world about which the hunters could have no knowledge. Both points of view have methodological dangers—subjective imprecision or objective imposition—and they are not really separable. It is very hard for anyone, scholars included, to be so completely and objectively aware of their own assumptions and ideological points of view that they know where emic turns into etic, and vice versa.

It is not surprising, given the above discussion, that historians relying, for the most part, on the equivocal and soft data of texts, have a greater ability or tendency to stress emic points of view; while archaeologists' material data leads to the more objective, etic points of view. And while these differing ideological positions can cause disagreements, especially about the reconstructed ideologies of the peoples studied, the potential for each to augment the knowledge of humankind and our past is great.

This book represents an historian's point of view by placing greater emphasis on eliciting the emic ideologies of the pyramid-builders. However, the material evidence, the shapes and construction techniques evidenced in the pyramids studied, is considered to be of vital importance in defining the emic point of view. Basically, hard data are "read," as texts might be for the subjective and equivocal traces of ideologies.

ADDRESSING THE PYRAMID

The following chapters use basic terms for discussing the pyramid, most of which, but not all, are commonly associated with the pyramid itself. However, if the ancient Egyptian pyramid is not treated as a paradigm for pyramid construction in general, then other descriptive terms must enter into the lexicon of pyramid terms.

Importantly, the pyramid is a form achieved by the massing of building material; any interior space is minimal or nonexistent. The shapes pyramids take are varied, but certainly not infinite. Their forms result from the combination of plan and elevation. Plans can be rectangular, circular, or square. Elevations rising from these plans often have battered profiles, stepped platforms, or geometric shapes. The battered profile, in architectural terms, refers to a wall that leans backwards from its base. Structurally, for an architecture of mass, it permits the achievement of greater height than a purely vertical wall could. Most stepped platforms use the battered profile as the "riser" between the horizontal steps, or stages. Following the diagonal batter to its top, each succeeding step or stage is smaller than the one below it. The best-known pyramidal shape, the geometric solid with a square base and triangular sides, obviously employs the battered profile. The other geometric shape is the curvilinear dome, or half-sphere of the stupa, an Indian religious structure comparable to pyramids by virtue of its monumentality, construction techniques, and its known functions.

The most general and widespread functions attributed to the pyramids that have been built are: as a burial site, as a monumental platform for a temple, and as a microcosmic form reiterating the larger cosmos, or macrocosmic universe. In this regard, all pyramids from all parts of the world traditionally have been referred to as holy mountains associated with the first acts of creation—although the creation story differs in particular histories and from place to place.

Only some architectural, but mostly practical, experience is needed to discuss the forms of pyramids. When archaeology has revealed their structural contexts and innards, then a discussion of pyramidal functions is a fairly obvious undertaking. More difficult, however, are the terms for discussing the ideas represented by the pyramids; but then this was the subject of the foregoing section on ideologies and points of view. However, in this regard, it is useful to consider how the ideas of the pyramids have influenced, and are still at play in, the modern imagination.

PYRAMIDS IN THE PRESENT

To study pyramids today is to study something foreign, forgotten, made by peoples long ago with whom our connection is slight in terms of language, culture, religion, and social and economic expectations. Conversely, pyramids are not just ancient curiosities. They are part of our present, they inhabit our spaces, and they remain as potent factors in our modern realities. How we think about and discuss pyramids reveals our assumptions about reality and aspirations for humanity, because we make many inferences about them based on the rigors of our modern disciplines.

One interesting assumption has to do with how we think the ancients thought. When we read their texts or excavate their pyramids and tombs, and especially when we use this evidence to reconstruct ancient concepts about life and death, religion and society, we do so according to how we think humankind has evolved in a particular time and place: the pyramids of Egypt are differently understood, because of their age and place, from the pyramids of Mesoamerica. But all early peoples, apparently, share a common characteristic in our estimation: their arts and architecture expressed meaning in structured, literal ways. I.E.S. Edwards in *Pyramids of Egypt* outlines the early Egyptian sun cult as it is described in the contemporary hieroglyphic texts of the Fifth and Sixth Dynasties (2465-2151 B.C.). Apparently divergent descriptions about how the sun moved across the sky—on a ship, carried by the wings of a falcon, or pushed by a scarab beetle—are characterized by Edwards as "schools of thought," or "theories," that contain "many inconsistencies". This assessment

of ancient Egyptian thought uses the (structural) terms, school of thought and theory, to describe what are more likely to be three poetic metaphors composed to describe the same thing. To consider any one of these descriptions as a "theory" about the sun's movements is to take literally the ancient Egyptians' metaphor. What could be more properly described as ancient theory would be illustrated by the consistency with which the Egyptian plans for the pyramid are laid out along the cardinal directions; a theory, perhaps, about how the smaller world of humankind can be positively aligned to the larger universe.

Modern thought has also created metaphors out of the pyramid, and these too are revealing. The forms of the pyramid still influence, through metaphor, modern architectural forms. The monumentality of the pyramids is likened to any project—regardless of form—perceived as having tremendous scope, requiring unheard-of amounts of funding, and resulting in very little obvious economic or social return.

At the end of the 18th century, the French architect Étienne-Louis Boullée designed a cenotaph for Sir Isaac Newton. Using simple geometric shapes, especially the sphere, the external massings of his memorial are a combination of stupa and the stepped stages of the ziggurat. The sphere was the monumental focus raised and supported by two circular stages planted with trees, perhaps emulating the Hanging Gardens of Babylon. The design of the sphere's interior space was inspired by Boullée's understanding of the ideology and function of the Egyptian pyramid—as a representation of the cosmos, but *here* defined by Newton, *and* as a symbolic burial with an empty sarcophagus duplicating what was found in the King's Chamber of the Great Pyramid.

The gigantic scale and aesthetic daring of Boullée's designs for memorials made most of them impossible actually to build during his lifetime. Even with today's building materials of steel and reinforced concrete, they would present immense technical problems, because they matched in size the ancient monuments that so stirred Boullée's imagination. Although almost forgotten during the 19th century, Boullée must be seen as a direct forerunner of the visionary architects of the early 20th century, especially Frank Lloyd Wright.

Wright did not employ the massive scale nor, certainly, the vertical dimension envisioned by Boullée: he was interested in designing domestic spaces, not cenotaphs. He was inspired by the ancient Mesoamerican pyramids of Mexico, especially by their "unitary" compositions of riser and step. His own designs,

Frank Lloyd Wright, the 20th-century American architect, was deeply influenced by the ancient pyramids of Mesoamerica. He specialized in designing domestic spaces in which his use of the horizontal dimension came into play. This is exemplified in Wright's Robie House, built in Chicago in 1907.

Reinforcing the premise that pyramids are not just ancient curiosities but also are part of our present, 20th-century architect I.M. Pei placed a transparent steel-and-glass pyramid in the courtyard of the Louvre Museum in Paris, where it contrasts strongly with its 16th-century surroundings.

such as the Robie House built in Chicago in 1907, demonstrate Wright's engagement with the horizontal dimension inspired by the stages of the ancient stepped pyramid.

The ancient monumental forms of the Egyptian pyramid, the Buddhist stupa, the stepped shapes of the Sumerian ziggurat, and the Mesoamerican platform have been, and will continue to be, the inspiration for architectural forms. The reasons have little to do with the actual monumentality of the structures, but because their formal simplicity is seen as ideologically, and thus metaphorically, monumental. Basic plans of squares, rectangles, and circles give rise to elevations of clear, uncomplicated profiles, and such forms are considered the goal of the modern architect seeking what is basic and archetypal to his art. It is here, however, that the relationship between the modern architect and the ancient pyramid becomes revealing. All modern architects design structures with interior spaces. Even Boullée, while he strived for the actual shape and monumentality of the ancient monuments, could not conceive of an architecture of mass. The modern architect, inspired by the ancient pyramid, looks to its plans and elevations, but seldom considers its mass as an important architectural feature. He objectifies, and thus changes, the actuality of the pyramid by making its impenetrable spaces transparent interiors. Today, anything built as mass is considered sculpture: for example, Robert Smithson's Spiral Jetty built into the Great Salt Lake of Utah. (To be fair, Frank Lloyd Wright did in fact dream of the beautiful buildings he could design if only it were not necessary to put in windows.)

The pyramid as a metaphor of simple, but complete, perfection is an aesthetic that can be traced to European understandings of the Egyptian pyramid

Like major monuments from earlier times, the mighty cathedrals of Europe required enormous resources and took many generations to build. They, too, were an expression of faith in a higher power, and housed the tombs of the nobility. The Cathedral of Reims in France is an example of Gothic design and workmanship at its most majestic.

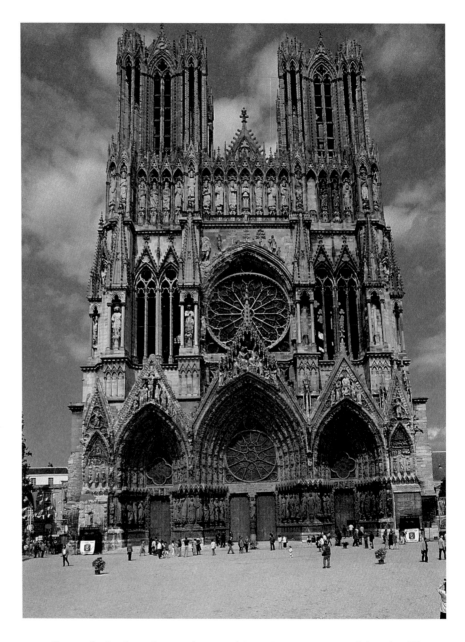

regardless of whether the modern architect is now inspired by the Khmer temple-towers or the ancient Mesoamerican stepped form. Beginning in the Age of Exploration during the 16th century, the Egyptian pyramid was used as a symbol for the actual as well as the philosophical expansion of the known European world: simple geometric shapes growing hugely out of unfamiliar landscapes; timeless, perfect, archetypal forms from the unknown dawn of humankind; places of wonder and pilgrimage. This is what inspires the modern architect, the primal perfection of the shapes and its evocation of times immemorial: the once and future form.

While of little interest to the modern architect, the tremendous mass making up the interior of the pyramid has become a metaphor for any undertaking seen as requiring superhuman effort and expenditures of energy over protracted periods of time—a multi-generational project. Art histories liken the construction of the Gothic cathedrals in western Europe to the building of the ancient pyramids, and more recently, the exploration of space has taken on the same metaphor. Indeed, Kurt Mendelssohn, in his book *The Riddle of the Pyramids*, proposes that, on an international scale, a space program requiring the spending of enormous resources and benefiting no one in particular could, if brilliantly organized, engender the need for cooperation that would transcend the destructive aspects of nationality that have plagued the world since the first states were, according to him, born out of the building of the first pyramids. It is the quest itself, not its results, that challenges and brings humankind into orderly, fruitful cooperation.

The analogy of the massive inner pyramid with other projects achieved through tremendous human effort originates from the same European interpretations and aesthetics as does the modern architect's use of its form. It is not the actualities of mass in the Egyptian pyramids that inspire modern reinterpretations of its functions, it is its seeming lack of functional necessity that compels us. The pyramid itself is not so important; the fact that it was built, however, is. If the object is a symbol of perfection, its mass becomes a visible symbol of human potential.

But what of the ancient American pyramid? Like the Egyptian, its forms have been reinterpreted, scaled down, and domesticated, but they serve as symbolic references to a different, non-European, past. Although the Mesoamerican and South American pyramids were first seen by Europeans at the same time as the burgeoning interest in Egyptian pyramids, the former never sparked the same kind of avid curiosity and attention until the 20th century. (The same is true for the Buddhist stupa, the Khmer temple-tower, and the ancient Chinese tumulus.) Even now, when we know the Mesoamerican pyramid functioned not only as a monumental marker but also as a place of burial, most scholars take great pains to make clear how different it is from its Egyptian counterpart—differences so often depicted in terms of what is lacking: the Mesoamerican pyramid lacks the same monumental scale, the durability of construction, and the perfection of a true geometry. Why the American pyramids did not, and actually still do not, arouse the close attention and imagination of the European mind is an intriguing question, and one whose answer has to do with what was stated in the preface to this book. The closed form of the ancient Egyptian pyramid has become a metaphor for perfection, while the meanings of the open form of the ancient Mesoamerican pyramid are still being investigated.

The temple of Angkor Wat in Cambodia reflects in its forms both Indian and Chinese architecture. Khmer temples were considered the residence the universe itself. To approach the complex, pilgrims must pass over a moat and then along a broad causeway that culminates in the massive

2

A BRIEF HISTORY OF PYRAMIDS

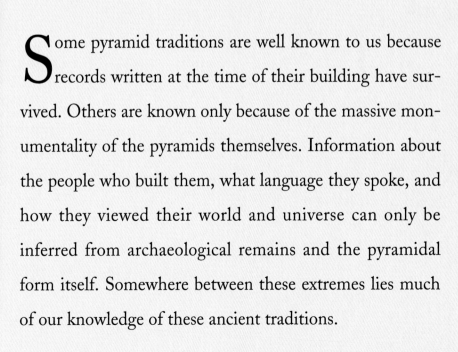

Some pyramid traditions are well known to us because records written at the time of their building have survived. Others are known only because of the massive monumentality of the pyramids themselves. Information about the people who built them, what language they spoke, and how they viewed their world and universe can only be inferred from archaeological remains and the pyramidal form itself. Somewhere between these extremes lies much of our knowledge of these ancient traditions.

of the deity and a microcosmic manifestation of pyramid terrace supporting the central tower.

The most telling similarities uniting all pyramid traditions, no matter how differently designed and used, are their massive evocation of mountains and the metaphoric functions they served in order to transform and connect: to transform the living and the dead; to connect nature, culture, and the cosmos.

ANCIENT SOUTH AMERICA

On the coast of Peru, during the fourth millennium B.C., the peoples of Aspero conceived of and were able to build massive monuments in the form of truncated pyramids. The first construction of these monuments, known dramatically as the Huaca de los Sacrificios and Huaca de los Idolos, has been dated to 3500 B.C. by radiocarbon methods. (The term *huaca* alludes to a sacred place of importance or a place of power and can be used to refer to something natural like a mountain, cave, or spring, or to something human-made, like a cairn or a temple.) Archaeologists characterize both of these monuments as platforms. On their top terraces, multiroomed structures were constructed and are thought to have been temples.

What is striking about the monuments at Aspero is where and when they were built. They were constructed on one of the driest coasts in the world by a people who had not yet participated in the Neolithic "invention" of fired pottery but were nonetheless living in settled towns or villages. Actually, very few peoples of the world were using fired pottery or living in settled villages at this early date. (Archaeological evidence shows fired pottery was being used by Neolithic peoples of Eastern Europe, the Near East, and the Far East during this period.) However, there was little agricultural activity along the coast of Peru at this time, given the region's desert-like climate. While some foods, such as squash and gourds, were domesticated, these ancient people were still engaged in foraging. Interestingly, they were also concerned with developing a sturdy cotton plant, not a foodstuff, for their industry and art of weaving. There seems little doubt that their vision of the world extended beyond bodily survival into what we would call the arts, but the question remains, how could the ancient peoples of Aspero have managed the necessary surpluses in human and economic energy necessary to achieve such monumental conceptions as their great platforms?

Michael Moseley, an archaeologist who has worked for many years along the Peruvian coast, believes that the rich abundance of the littoral region—and, possibly, of the open sea—furnished these early peoples with enough protein to maintain a settled existence. Whether Moseley is right or wrong, and there are some who disagree with his characterization of preceramic life, the fact is that ancient Aspero was not inhabited by nomadic hunters and gatherers, as archaeology tells us most Native Americans were at this time. They managed somehow to create enough energy (human, economic, cultural, or otherwise) to cause astounding, mountain-like monuments to rise from the coastal desert.

The pyramid mound of Huaca de los Idolos, at Aspero, Peru, dates from the fourth millennium B.C., and is the first known monumental pyramid to have been built. Shown here from the north during excavations, the pyramid was constructed by a unique, bag-fill method: bags woven from grasses were filled with rubble and were then used as "building blocks."

And they built these monuments in a unique manner, using what is called net-bag fill. This means that bags were woven—twined really—from reedy grasses into nets that would hold approximately a half-bushel. Each net bag would be filled with rubble and used to construct the immense mass of the pyramid. The bags were not used for transporting rubble fill, but as "building blocks." How many thousands—hundreds of thousands—of bags were needed for such a monumental construction? Another building material used, sun-dried adobe brick, is much more common for desert architecture. The adobes were formed in an interesting shape—that of a cone—and were laid either vertically or horizontally in geometric patterns. The adobes were used either as facing material or as heartings for the construction of walls and were ultimately covered with smooth stucco or a mud plaster.

The fact is that Huaca de los Sacrificios and Huaca de los Idolos are the first known monumental pyramids to have been conceived and built, and thus must have the honor of beginning this brief history. However, we know little about their builders other than that they could, and did, build such monuments.

Later, during the first millennium B.C., the ancient peoples of Chavín de Huántar, located in the northern Andean highlands of Peru, constructed a remarkable pyramidal monument. Sequentially constructed over several hundred years, the Temple Complex of Chavín de Huántar was built of stone blocks, as might be expected for a mountainous region. It was architecturally designed to promote what can be understood only as water ceremonies.

The pyramid monument of Chavín de Huántar in the Andean highlands of Peru was constructed over a period of several hundred years and seems to have been designed for water ceremonies.

Within the mass of the Old and the New Temples that make up the Temple Complex, water channels were built, as well as narrow, labyrinthine passages. The function of the passages is unknown; perhaps they were used for initiatory rites. But the channels clearly were used ritually, with water caused to flow around and within the temples to effect proper symbolic or metaphoric purposes. Furthermore, as it coursed through the channels, the water would make sounds. One can imagine sonorous drips and gurgles or, as one archaeologist supposes, water rushing through the channels to make the whole temple roar.

The carved Lanzon Slab—depicting a part human, part serpent, part caiman creature—is thought to represent a major deity of the people who built the Temple Complex of Chavín de Huántar. The 13-foot-high (4-meter-high) sculpture stands at the crossing point of two passageways in the Old Temple.

Within the center, the heart of the massive Old Temple, an extraordinary sculpture, shaped like a stalactite and measuring roughly 13 feet (3.9 meters) in height, was placed at the crossing of two passageways, where it marks the vertical and central axes of the Old Temple. Known as the Lanzon Slab, or the Great Image, it portrays in continuous, shallow relief an anthropomorphic creature, the "Smiling God"—part human, part serpent, part caiman—thought to be a major deity of the ancient peoples who built Chavín de Huántar. Axially positioned, this sculpture inhabited a cave-like space in a human-made mountain where water ran through carefully constructed channels. Perhaps this elaborate and artful staging represents and conjures energies and forces known to exist in nature, but not naturally experienced in any manifest order. Certainly, however, the associ-

Stones of tremendous mass and size were used in the construction of the stepped terraces of Sacsahuamán (*below*). These pose the question of exactly how they were shaped and fitted together with such precision. Each stone fits perfectly between its neighbors without the use of mortar. Inca stonemasons shaped the stones so that they protrude at the center, giving the pillow-like effect that is visible on Cuzco's famed "Stone of Twelve Angles" (*right*).

ated ideas of mountain, cave, world-axis, and water join the Temple Complex of Chavín de Huántar to most other pyramid traditions.

About 80 years before the conquistador Francisco Pizarro arrived in the city of Cuzco, during the reign (1438-1471) of the great and ambitious Inca, Pachacuti Yupanqui, construction was begun on what is now called the Fortress of Sacsahuamán at the northeastern end of Cuzco. The nature of its original function or functions is not clear to us, but some scholars hold that Sacsahuamán was a religious place associated with sun-worship. That it had a dual function as a temple-fortress, however, is the most common interpretation of this phenomenal construction.

Many, perhaps, would not regard Sacsahuamán as a pyramid. Much of its original construction is now lost, because it was used as a quarry for the building of colonial Cuzco; yet what remains, including stepped terraces, is in itself so monumental that it is hard to forego its presence here.

It exhibits design features that suggest water rituals, like the Temple Complex of Chavín de Huántar, but more importantly, Sacsahuamán manifests unique and sophisticated conceptions about architecture and its place in the natural world.

Sacsahuamán exemplifies ancient ideals for architecture that can be properly called "topographic enhancement." Situated on a hill with large rocky protrusions, the building of Sacsahuamán incorporates—really marries—human constructions and natural features. The whole hill is an architectural monument because of the additions, insertions, and alterations achieved through human mediation or "enhancement." Incaic concepts and philosophies about the relationships between nature and culture—an age-old human problem—are revealed in an architecture used to mediate between humankind and the world in which they lived. It does not seem such mediation was conceived primarily as protection and shelter from natural forces, but as a kind of exploration. Natural forms were not obliterated, nor were they left unchanged. Built structures do not blend into the landscape as modern romantic ideals for architectural success would dictate, they are formally evident. They seem to place an exploratory line between the natural and the cultural, and where architecture meets nature—block to rock, smooth to rough, color to color—the meeting is vivid and energetic, but not hierarchical. Nature never overcomes the built, nor does the built deny or overpower its place.

The stepped terraces partially surrounding and leading up to structures on the topmost elevation of the natural hill are, perhaps, the most impressive and best-known features of Sacsahuamán—or, for that matter, of ancient Cuzco. Sawtoothed in the outline of their plan, each terrace is retained by a wall of stones composed in what students of Incaic architecture call polygonal coursing. This term refers to the fact that each stone is carefully shaped and dressed with several odd sides and is thus polygonal. Nonetheless, each is fitted perfectly with its several neighbors in a drywall technique without the use of mortar. As the facing surface of each stone reaches its various edges, it is gently curved inward so that where the stones actually meet there is a slight recession behind the vertical surface of the wall. Each stone appears to be compressed by its neighbors so that its surface bulges and so that its material actuality as hard stone seems redefined in some way by this "pillowing" effect. The wall surfaces, then, are visually very lively with irregular and eccentric shapes defined by textures of light and shadow.

It is the enormous scale on which these effects are achieved that is so magnificent. The revetment or retaining walls of the sawtoothed terraces at Sacsahuamán use stones of tremendous mass and size. Although supposedly built in 50 years, the question of how the ancient architects and stonemasons could have worked with such precision on so monumental a scale has never been answered. Several theories have been offered, but none are convincing. The most generally cited theory envisions a scaffolding of timber with rope swings. One of the contingent blocks would be swung by the ropes against its neighbor laid on the ground. By means of sand and friction, the swinging block would rub against its counterpart until perfectly fitting edges were achieved. For polygonal coursing, this would necessitate several "swings" of different orientation for each block, and for the revetment stones at Sacsahuamán, the engineering of the scaffolding would have had to accommodate stones weighing from several to hundreds of tons. Fifty years?

Pedro de Cieza de León, a 16th-century chronicler, provides the best, more or less contemporary, information about Sacsahuamán. At least 20,000 workers, from foremen to quarriers, were employed in the construction at the hill of Sacsahuamán. The architects and designers were Huallpa Rimachi, Maricanchi,

Acahuana, and Calla Cunchui, all supposedly Inca nobles. Started in the reign of Pachacuti, it was finished 50 years later by his son and successor, Inca Topac Yupanqui. Another 16th-century chronicler, Garcilaso de la Vega, who used to play in the ruins of Sacsahuamán as a boy, relates that the structures "guarded" by the sawtoothed revetments were palaces, towers, temples, and storehouses. Like the Temple Complex of Chavín de Huántar, it was a place of water ceremonies with pools and channels for the running and gathering—perhaps storage—of water. A prominent round structure, seen today as if in a plan marked out by stones, was the likely focus of watery rituals. Garcilaso de la Vega says it was a tower that descended into the ground as far as it ascended to the sky. This seems apocryphal but may retain some vestige of the *axis mundi*, or world pivot concept.

The round structure was built of beautifully cut stones in what is called regular coursing, supposedly reserved for the most revered and sacred buildings. Unlike polygonal coursing, regularly cut blocks would be of even height along one course, although not always of even width. The blocks would be recessed at the meeting joints, but the pillowing effect was much more subtle than that used for polygonal coursing. More even, regular, and geometrically perfect in shape, regularly coursed walls would not have required the same time and energy needed to fit and course the jigsaw shapes of polygonal coursing.

Throughout and around the hill of Sacsahuamán, evocative shapes are worked within and onto the natural rock. These are often called huacas, the Inca's Throne being a good example. The rock has been smoothed and cut into a series of "steps" where emphasis is given to vertical and horizontal rhythms. The scale is not that of furniture, nor that of architecture. The Inca's Throne is clearly meaningful, but it just as clearly lacks any ascertainable function. Perhaps its meaning relates to an exploratory mediation between culture and nature.

That a pyramid was understood by the peoples who built it as an effigy of the holy mountain, axially located in the center of the world, is almost universal. Embellishing the holy mountain with a cave and a water source seems reasonable and, indeed, it is a common metaphoric extension. The affinities between water, mountains, and caves, and their perceived connectedness evidenced by the design of the Temple Complex of Chavín de Huántar and the Fortress of Sacsahuamán, are also to be found in the pyramid traditions of China and Southeast Asia. Caves will be seen to be an important adjunct to the ancient Mesoamerican idea of pyramid, while water may have played a more important role within the Old Kingdom Egyptian pyramid tradition than is usually recognized.

ANCIENT MESOAMERICA

Within the native civilizations of the American continents, traditions for building pyramids that more closely resemble the way pyramids are *supposed* to look were developed in Mesoamerica, a territory which includes the countries of Mexico, Guatemala, Belize, and the northern parts of El Salvador and

The Olmec ceremonial complex of La Venta, located near the Gulf Coast of Mexico, consists of a northern and a southern group of ceremonial structures separated by a pyramid of tamped earth 100 feet (30 meters) in height. The pyramid, or effigy volcano, represents the earliest known structure of its kind in Mesoamerica.

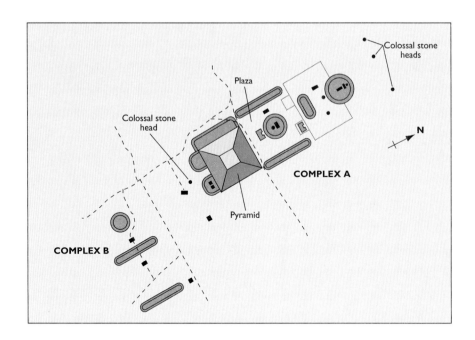

Honduras. Mesoamerican pyramids were constructed from the first millennium B.C. until the Conquest of the early 16th century and participated in the universal conception that the pyramid was an effigy of a mountain and, as with the South American examples, expressed conceptual linkages between mountain and cave. Unlike South American pyramidal platforms, however, there is little evidence to be found in the archaeological literature to suggest that water rituals were associated with their Mesoamerican counterparts.

One of the earliest known pyramids in Mesoamerica was built between 1000-400 B.C. by the ancient Olmec peoples for the ceremonial complex of La Venta, located in the modern Mexican state of Tabasco, near the Gulf Coast. Although archaeologists have not ascertained its constructional history, the pyramid appears to have been formed by tamped earth and faced with clay to emulate the shape of a volcano, conical in elevation and apparently irregularly fluted in plan. Because it is constructed of tamped earth, however, the possibility remains that its irregular plan, rising in ridges to the top, may be the result of natural erosion processes. Indeed, until Robert Heizer's investigations of the pyramid in the 1950s, this was the general opinion. Heizer, however, considers that the fluting was part of the intentional, original design, and his arguments are good ones, especially concerning the regularity of the flutes.

Although we have as yet no reason to believe that the pyramid was constructed to participate in water ceremonies, as pyramids were in South America, some such ceremonials may well have taken place at La Venta. Carefully constructed drainpipes have been found in the ceremonial area south of the pyramid, and while they may have served the necessary functional pur-

The irregular, fluted shape of the La Venta pyramid is possibly due to the effects of centuries of erosion, but the fluting may also have been the intention of its Olmec builders. Archaeological investigation of the interior of the tamped-earth mound has indicated the presence of a rectangular structure just below the summit.

pose of draining excess water from terraced surfaces, more drainpipes were found at the nearby and perhaps earlier Olmec site of San Lorenzo in contexts usually described as ceremonial or ritual.

The effigy volcano, rising approximately 100 feet (30 meters) above the alluvial coastal lands, was centrally placed between two ceremonial complexes. Complex A, to the north of the pyramid, was carefully aligned along a north-south axis (eight degrees west of north), and was almost totally destroyed in the early 1960s when an airstrip was constructed to assist oil-drilling activities. South of the pyramid is a less-defined ceremonial area known as Complex B, or the Stirling Group, after Matthew Stirling, a pioneer archaeologist in the Olmec region. The north-south axis, so important for Complex A, can only be detected in the alignment of some of the many monuments found here. More surveying needs to be done to have a clearer picture of the relationship between the Stirling Group, the pyramid, and the northern complex. The pyramid, however, is squarely aligned with the prominent axis of the northern Complex A and is thought to face in that direction.

It can be supposed, but not archaeologically proven, that the pyramid marks a burial, or burials, of anciently important people, because several important burials were found laid along the ceremonial axis within Complex A and because of suggestive magnetometer readings. These readings can also be interpreted as revealing a possible rectangular substructure within 10 to 33 feet (3 to 10 meters) of the top of the pyramid, which may be a small temple built at or near the top. This speculation offers the only reference to the metaphoric cave—an aspect that is otherwise missing from this first example of an ancient Mesoamerican pyramid. Such a temple would not preclude the presence of a burial or burials.

Mound construction, or the tamped-earth technique, is characteristic of ancient Olmec architectural methods and materials used for ceremonial, civic, and religious purposes. The usual function for tamped-earth construction was as a platform for less permanent sheltering spaces built of wattle-and-daub walls with thatched roofs. These would be both humble dwellings and, in the ceremonial centers, small temples atop larger, more impressive platforms. Within a swampy, alluvial landscape, such platforms would have a practical purpose. Thus, in Mesoamerica, domestic architectural forms (and solutions) were expanded and enlarged, but not materially changed, to create the first examples of ceremonial or civic architecture. (The secular source for ceremonial architectural forms is also reflected in later ceremonial plans wherein three or four temples face into a common courtyard like structures in domestic compounds still do today.)

Given these reflections on the formal sources and functions of tamped-earth architecture, the pyramid of La Venta stands out as a significant or, in its time, unique expression of ideas about monumental form. No trace of a ramp or stair leading to its top has been detected, giving the impression that the conical, fluted pyramid is more like sculpture than architecture, albeit in monumental, or architectural, scale.

If the pyramid at La Venta can be considered an essentially sculptural effigy of a volcano rendered in a one-to-one scale, then the better-known monumental sculptures created by the ancient Olmecs must be mentioned. These are the great and colossal heads carved from basalt blocks weighing many tons and found throughout the ancient Olmec heartland (now considered to be, for the most part, the modern states of Veracruz and Tabasco). At La Venta, four such heads were found in locations suggesting they functioned as "guardians" of the ceremonial center: three heads facing north, aligned perpendicularly across the central axis and just north of Complex A, and one head facing south, placed on the central axis just south of or behind the effigy-pyramid. Bodiless, the giant heads appear to represent the unique features of portraits because each head is carved with different and distinct physiognomical and psychological features.

In their monumentality, these heads represent similar but not identical ideas or concepts about sculptural scale to those of the pyramid at La Venta. The pyramid is an effigy of a volcano carved on a one-to-one scale—a mountain re-created by emulating its own and proper scale. As an idea, this re-creation of a

Situated close to the diminished pyramid at La Venta are four finely preserved basalt sculptures of human heads. Although bodiless, they represent humanity on a monumental scale: if given bodies, they would stand almost 50 feet (15 meters) tall. The detail of the facial expressions gives each head a definite personality, but the enormity of their scale is without precedent.

With the magnificent Pyramid of the Sun rising above it, Teotihuacán was the preeminent city of Central Mexico from the last century B.C. to about the eighth century A.D. At its height, the city covered 7.7 square miles (20 square kilometers), and supported a population of at least 125,000 people. The Pyramid of the Sun, seen in the foreground, has five terraced platforms. It is believed that a temple once stood atop it. Its rise in elevation seems to indicate an access to the heavens, while its orientation reflects solar and celestial cycles.

mountain in, or close to, its own scale is how most pyramids throughout the world are described. But in context with the gigantic heads, the ancient Olmec concept of world or holy mountain becomes more specific and unique. The heads represent humanity on a monumental scale—an enlargement that reaches toward the fantastic. What is of interest here has to do with human scale and human perception of the world. When we look at a mountain, we are awed by the enormity of nature and its forces; when we look at a constructed, human-made mountain, we are awed for different reasons—the enormity of human aspirations and the possibilities for human achievement. In either situation, human-made or natural, the mountain elicits an understandable sense of grandness, because of the natural differences in scale between the human body and the vast mass of the mountain/pyramid. The gigantic heads carved by the ancient Olmec undo this natural scale difference. If these heads were given bodies, the figures would stand close to 50 feet (15.2 meters) in height and be half as tall as the pyramid. The scale relationship between the Olmec heads and the pyramid is similar to that of a human standing next to a two-story building—not generally understood as an awe-inspiring difference in scale. What vision, what understanding of the world, was behind this unique Olmec ordering of scale? How do we understand the heads? They look so human we can believe they have personalities. In their furrowed brows, we read a history of human success and failure, and indeed, they are generally thought to be portraits of local rulers. If so, in their aggrandized and awesome scale, they appear beyond human definition, perhaps deities rendered at proper scale and as potent as nature...but their expressions, their faces, are so human. It is an enigma, but surely the question of scale is important in the understanding of the ancient Olmec pyramid. (It is possible that their seeming humanity is the result not of standing before the sculptures themselves, but of studying photographs of these sculptures, such as the one in this book, which is measurable by inches, and wherein only traces of the overwhelming scale and mass of these sculptures can be detected.)

In central Mexico, not far from Mexico City, the great city of Teotihuacán flourished from the beginnings of our present era until the seventh or eighth century. We are not certain who the ancient builders of this city were or what language they spoke, but they were great builders of pyramids. Perhaps one of the most famous pyramids of all Mesoamerica is the Pyramid of the Sun, built early in the history of Teotihuacán between A.D. 1 and 250. How the peoples of ancient Teotihuacán may have related to, or have been influenced by, the earlier Olmecs is little understood. As will become apparent in the following description of the Teotihuacán pyramid, there are differences in material, construction, shape, and perhaps conception.

In comparison to the La Venta pyramid, the inner construction of the Pyramid of the Sun has not been thoroughly investigated, but our knowledge of its outer construction is much greater. The pyramid rises from a square plan with each side measuring approximately 730 feet (220 meters) at the base. In elevation it originally rose to an estimated height of about 200 feet (60.5 meters) and is divided into five stepped terraces. Presumably, the top terrace supported a temple made of more perishable materials, but evidence for or against such a reconstruction is now lost. A grand staircase rises up the west face. Archaeological tunnels dug along the east-west axis of the pyramid have led investigators to speculate that a tomb of immense proportions was constructed of adobe bricks and located at the very center of the pyramid's foundations.

The pyramid was constructed of rubble-fill and probably initially was faced with adobe bricks. These were covered with a cobblestone facing set in mortar, which is the pyramid we see today. Originally, the Pyramid of the Sun had two other "skins," another stone facing and a final stucco coating, but these were mostly lost during the 1905-10 excavations undertaken to ready the great pyramid for President Porfirio Díaz's centennial commemoration of Mexico's independence from Spain. The use of dynamite was an acceptable technique for excavation at the turn of the century, and it is estimated that the perimeter of the pyramid could have been lessened by as much as 23 feet (7 meters) in some places.

It is generally considered that this great pyramid was designed and constructed in one continuous effort, lasting about 50 years. However, nothing in the archaeological record prohibits proposing that the two stone facings (one now lost) that covered the so-called "hidden pyramid" of adobe and rubble-fill were added as later enlargements and improvements and were not necessarily conceived as parts of the original design and construction.

There is a great deal of empirical evidence that the designers of the great Pyramid of the Sun were exceedingly mindful about the placement of its mass and the arrangement of its elevated profiles. By its location, orientation, and design, the pyramid metaphorically manifests ideas concerning the three vertical levels of the ancient Mesoamerican cosmos: the celestial, the terrestrial, and the subterranean (or chthonic). In 1972, while excavating at the front of the pyramid around an apron-like structure called an *adosada* that fronts the pyramid, archaeologists discovered the entrance to a cave that ran under the pyramid to its center. The cave, when explored, proved to be a natural one whose shape had been enhanced just enough to make it look like the place of mythical origins and emergence we know pictured in Conquest-period chronicles; that is, an underground pathway leading out from four apsidal chapels arranged like the petals of a flower. Clearly, one function of the pyramid was to mark this place of underworld power.

Archaeoastronomers have determined that the odd orientation of the Street of the Dead, or the central, ceremonial axis of Teotihuacán, is related to celestial events that are also signaled by the Pyramid of the Sun, whose stairway is perpendicular to the street. By standing on the stairway and looking across the Street to the far horizon (approximately 15 degrees north of west), the archaeoastronomer Anthony Aveni calculated one would have seen in the year A.D. 150 the zenith sunset, having just been preceded by the setting of the

44

Lined by numerous temples and shrines, the Street of the Dead is the central ceremonial axis of Teotihuacán. It leads past the Pyramid of the Sun toward the mountains on the western edge of the Valley of Mexico. The pyramid's massive profile seems to have been influenced by distant Mount Patlachique, whose shape and contour it closely resembles.

Pleiades. Furthermore, located on Cerro Colorado about four miles (6.4 kilometers) west of Teotihuacán is an ancient marker aligned on this perpendicular sight-line. Thus, while we generally feel that the great rise and elevation of the Pyramid of the Sun aspires to create access to the heavens, its orientation also reflects celestial movements and cycles.

Most efforts to discover the terrestrial meanings of the pyramid are problematic, in that they are based on measurement and number and have elicited several theories concerning how its numbers relate to geometric and cosmic proportions. As discussed above, the actual measurements of the pyramid were lost to faulty excavation techniques, and all theories that relate number to cosmic dimensions must base their numbers on reconstructed measurements. Such work tends to be tautological or circular in logic: if the basic unit of measurement is n, then the base of the pyramid would measure 365 x n. That is to say, the reconstructed measurement seems to confirm the proposed unit; but in fact, the unit itself is derived from this reconstruction.... The point here is not to debunk such efforts, but until more secure data is achieved, they must be considered theoretical.

However, other questions concerning the terrestrial meanings of the pyramid can be asked. Just how this monumental structure relates to the world (not to the underworld or the heavens but its place in normal experience) must have to do with the pyramid's mountainous scale, its five terraced platforms, and its function as a focus for public activity, both religious and secular, within the city.

The scale and location of the pyramid are important considerations. In the first place, the pyramid is located within a city; indeed, its presence can be seen and felt throughout the vast area that has been identified as the "city limits" of Teotihuacán by the survey project headed by the archaeologist René Millon. Certainly a number of other, earlier pyramids (some just discussed) were built within centers, but whether these were true cities or simply ceremonial centers has long been a matter of debate. There is no doubt about Teotihuacán's status as a city. This point may seem obvious enough, but it is an important distinction among various pyramid-building traditions, and indicates differing conceptions about function. Some, like the ancient Egyptian pyramids, were situated outside villages or cities and thus outside secular and civic spaces. Thus, however we wish to categorize the activities that took place on and around the Pyramid of the Sun—religious and/or secular—these activities took place within the civic and mostly public context of a city. Part of its meaning and function was as a civic monument.

Although seldom mentioned in writings about the Pyramid of the Sun, an "alignment" is often imaged in photographs taken of the pyramid from the obvious vantage point of the northernmost pyramid at Teotihuacán, the Pyramid of the Moon. Here one can look south along the axis of the Street of the Dead and see, as the photographs show, the Pyramid of the Sun's massive scale and sloping profile reiterating the mass and slope of Mount Patlachique, which defines the western edge of the Valley of Mexico. Most tourists comment on this reiteration; it is a visual "event" that is hard to miss.

Whether or not the designers of the pyramid intended this kind of reiteration or reflection between nature and human-made forms, it happened, and surely was acknowledged as such in ancient times as it is today. The reflection gives greater potency to the purposes of the pyramid as we can detect them: as an entrance to the cave of origins, perhaps a place of burial, as a marker for the zenith sun, as the marker that in fact orients the grid-plan of the city, and as a "natural" reiteration of the world in which it was built. The Pyramid of the Sun does more than just evoke or represent the celestial, the terrestrial, and the infernal realms, it marks and commemorates the very place where these realms have "naturally" come together.

Although Teotihuacán's source of wealth and power is thought to have been its control of ancient obsidian mining and distribution, the city was also a major center of pilgrimage. Later Mexica (Aztec) beliefs that Teotihuacán was the place

The Temple of Inscriptions at Palenque, in the Mexican state of Chiapas, takes its name from the three carved limestone tablets found in the temple structure atop the nine-stage stepped pyramid.

"where the gods were born" and the world began are borne out by the circumstances just described for the Pyramid of the Sun: that ancient people came to the pyramid of Teotihuacán, where people still are drawn today.

Turning to the tropical lowlands of southern Mesoamerica, the pyramid that best exemplifies the function of burial is the Temple of Inscriptions built at Palenque for the great Maya ruler Pacal. The pyramid probably was begun sometime after the middle of the seventh century A.D., under Pacal's patronage, and finished at the end of that century or in the early years of the eighth century under Pacal's son, Chan Bahlum. It is a stepped pyramid of nine stages surmounted by a temple designed in the typical manner of Palenque—piers decorated with stuccoed imagery, a sloping, battered cornice, and a graceful roof comb, now mostly lost, rising from the centerline of the slightly pitched roof. Within the rooms of the temple were found three limestone tablets each carved with a long hieroglyphic inscription, hence the name, Temple of Inscriptions.

The 1952 excavation of a stairway leading from the floor of the shrine atop the Temple of Inscriptions deep into the heart of the structure led to the discovery of the tomb of the Maya ruler Pacal. The find identified the pyramid as a memorial for the departed ruler.

The 1952 excavation of a stairway leading from the floor of the shrine atop the Temple of Inscriptions deep into the heart of the structure led to the discovery of the tomb of the Maya ruler Pacal. The find identified the pyramid as a memorial for the departed ruler.

Between 1948 and 1952, the great Mexican archaeologist Alberto Ruz Lhullier uncovered an extraordinary tomb approached by stairs descending from the upper temple into the hearting of the pyramid to just below ground level, under the center of the pyramid's mass. Because the stairs had to have been constructed as the mass of the pyramid was being raised, there can be no question about the importance of the pyramid's function as a marker for the tomb of Pacal.

The stairway was constructed as a series of descending (or ascending) corbeled vaults—13 in all. As the nine exterior terraces of the pyramid refer in cosmic numerology to the nine underworld levels, the number 13 evokes the 13 levels of heaven. The pyramid formally reverses the logic of the cosmos. One ascends the nine platforms as if descending to the underworld cave of origins (the temple at the top of the pyramid). And then, within the pyramid, one descends to the tomb beneath the pyramid as if ascending the 13 levels of heaven to its utmost elevation. If the ascending and descending journeys were reversed and taken as starting from the burial, then one (the deceased Pacal?) would walk up the 13 levels to the heaven at the top of the mountain, but down the nine levels to the lowest subterranean level, which must be the plaza floor.

It is clear and generally accepted that the Pyramid of Inscriptions represents a cosmogram, but that it potentially reverses, or makes equivocal, conceptual logic is also of interest and may suggest that the pyramid was conceived as a place outside normal, existential realities—a mirror-world, the holy mountain. One rises to the depths and descends to heights, and reality is a proposition of apposites.

48

The corbel-vaulted burial chamber below the Temple of Inscriptions at Palenque measures 30 feet by 13 feet (9 meters by 4 meters). Much of the area of the chamber is taken up by the thick stone slab visible in this photograph. Underneath the slab, the jade-covered remains of Pacal were found entombed in a stone box.

There is a quality of philosophical delectation embedded in the Palenque pyramid, an intellectualism that can be associated with certain of the ancient Maya peoples and cities during their periods of ascendancy (A.D. 200-800). However, it is not a normal characteristic of ancient Mesoamerican thought and philosophy, which generally tends toward greater literalism and pragmatism. These qualities can be seen and adduced from the Mexica (Aztec) pyramid built

The partially restored pyramid at Tenayuca, in a suburb of Mexico City, is one of the largest surviving Aztec structures. The two stairways rose to the top platform, where twin temples once stood. These were probably made of perishable materials, and have not survived. The pyramid was enlarged eight times following its initial construction in the 13th century, and probably served as a model for the Templo Mayor at Tenochtitlán.

at the ancient site of Tenayuca, northwest of modern Mexico City. This edifice is an excellent example for illustrating an important feature of the Mesoamerican pyramid, which is to say, constant rebuilding and remodeling.

The pyramid of Tenayuca was designed with an approximately square plan and rises in elevation by four staged platforms with sloping profiles. On the west face of this massive platform, a grand, double stairway ascends to the top platform that once supported twin temples reflecting the double stairs. The first pyramid was probably constructed at the end of the 13th century and is (as revealed by archaeologist's tunnels) a small version of the pyramid that can be seen today, which was probably completed sometime late in the 15th century. During this period of three centuries, the pyramid was rebuilt eight times, six of which were major enlargements of the previous structure. (The other two rebuilding projects were really small remodelings of previous stages.) The basic plan and elevation of the pyramid, while enlarged or embellished, remained the same as described above. The final pyramid sits on a low and wide platform on

At the heart of the ritual precinct of the Aztec capital of Tenochtitlán lay the Templo Mayor, a massive pyramid shown here in a model reconstruction. Surmounting the pyramid were the shrines to Tláloc, the rain god, and to Huitzilopochtli, the patron deity of the Mexica. As the very center of the Aztec world, the temple combined images of both fertility and warfare. This was reflected as much by the offerings placed within its walls during construction as by the human sacrifices that took place before the altar of Huitzilopochtli.

which sculptured serpents, linked together, surround the pyramid on all sides, except on the western side with the balustraded stairs.

Because of the number of rebuilding projects, however, it has been postulated that these took place for ritual rather than structural reasons. Six major enlargements over a period of 300 years would mean one every 50 years. This is so close to the important time cycle of 52 years in the ancient Mesoamerican calendar, that it is very reasonable to consider the ritual rebuildings to have been timed by this cycle.

The more famous Templo Mayor of Tenochtitlán, recently excavated in the center of modern Mexico City, is very much like the Tenayuca pyramid: oriented toward the west with double stairways and temples and rebuilt or remodeled in eight different projects, beginning sometime in the early 14th century. The twin temples of the Templo Mayor pyramid were dedicated to the war god, Huitzilopochtli, the ancestral hero/deity of the Mexica, and to Tláloc, an ancient fertility deity primarily associated with water. It seems likely that the Tenayuca pyramid was endowed with similar significance, that is, the pairing of an ancestral, dynastic hero/deity with a more ancient, agricultural and subterranean deity, a duality eloquently described by the art historian Richard Townsend in his article, "Pyramid and Sacred Mountain." In a sense, the later Mexica pyramids place two worlds or realities next to each other, rather than within one another as at Palenque. Apposition is literally manifested and illustrated by the two temples. In ascending the stairs, one ascends four platforms and reaches, not the apogee nor the nadir, but the center of the cosmos defined as the center of the four cardinal directions and as two, apposite principles, humanity and nature.

No major burials have so far been found within either the Tenayuca pyramid or the Templo Mayor, although in the latter, over 50 buried offerings have been found. These offerings were made to honor and mark the rebuilding projects. One of these, Offering No. 48, holds the bones and skulls of children, and is considered not so much a burial as cached evidence of child sacrifice. At Tenayuca and later at Tenochtitlán, every generation would see their main pyramid redefined, remodeled, or enlarged. Mexica pyramids were places of almost constant building activity.

AFRICAN AND NEAR EASTERN PYRAMIDS

The only traits that seem to link the Egyptian pyramids and the ziggurats of Mesopotamia are square plans, impressive elevations, and the religious or metaphoric meaning of mountain. In other respects, they are very different in their placement, forms, functional uses, and building materials. In fact, because of its placement within the city and its formation by stepped terraces, the Mesopotamian pyramid is closer to the ancient pyramids of Mesoamerica than it is to its more contemporary and geographically nearer neighbor, Egypt. This insight was proposed by the French writer André Malraux, in his searching preface to André Parrot's *Sumer, The Dawn of Art*. The fact is, as briefly touched on in the preface, when considered within the context of world traditions of pyramid building, the Egyptian pyramid of the Fourth Dynasty (2584-2465 B.C.) is unique.

This uniqueness has to do with its form as a monumental, geometric form and how such a shape really discourages human participation. In other respects, the Egyptian pyramid positively compares with the diverse traditions of pyramid building, such as being described as the holy mountain at the center of the world, functioning as a burial place, and reflecting cardinal directions and celestial orders.

The history of the Egyptian pyramid, as we now understand it, suggests that it derives from a common desire to mark burials of important people with a structure that also serves as a monumental sign for community and communal events. Mastabas first marked royal burials, dating from predynastic times and continuing as a viable form well into the Dynastic period of the Old Kingdom (circa 3000-2100 B.C.). In its own history of development, the mastaba is thought to make more permanent an ephemeral pile of earth that originally marked the early Neolithic pit-burials of Egypt. Even in those early times, such a pile probably was considered a sacred symbol for the mound of earth that protruded out of the muds of chaos at the beginning of time, an event repeated yearly when the receding flood waters of the Nile reveal mounds of enriched earth. As the scientist and writer Kurt Mendelssohn suggests, the early marker-piles may have been the inspiration for the formal shape of the later pyramids and thereby suggest the symbolic connotations of creation and rebirth; one has only to imagine the natural pyramidal shape that a pile of sand assumes.

The form of the Egyptian mastaba was derived from predynastic times, when a mound of earth was raised to mark the burial of a ruler. The mastaba was a flat-roofed brick structure that marked the grave of a ruler as a dwelling for his spirit. By the Fifth or Sixth Dynasty, when this example was built, the mastaba was no longer reserved solely for royal burials, and consisted of numerous rooms, corridors, and halls.

After the Fourth Dynasty, the mastaba is not commonly used for royal burials and is associated instead with lesser officials and members of the royal household, reflecting, perhaps, a growing number of class divisions within ancient Egyptian society. The mastaba is formed from a rectangular plan and a plain-walled elevation. It is seldom monumental, traditionally being conceived within the scale of domestic architecture and, like domestic architecture, built with adobe brick. Indeed, the word "mastaba" derives from an Arabic word for bench, a convenient architectural feature built out from the walls of domestic houses. After the Third Dynasty, however, the architecture of royal burials eludes any suggestion of domestic, familiar forms. (Paintings and sculptures associated with royal burials often depict daily life, but the fact is that the architectural forms themselves do not.)

The burial complex of King Zoser (Neterkhet) of the Third Dynasty (2584-2568 B.C.) at Saqqara includes the first imaginative enlargement of the mastaba into a stepped pyramid. The ancient Egyptians credited Imhotep,

The funeral chamber of the Pyramid of Unas, at Saqqara, near Memphis in Egypt, was the first in which the interior walls were covered with religious and magic inscriptions. Similar texts appear inside other royal pyramid-tombs of the Fifth and Sixth dynasties at Saqqara.

the king's architect, with this extension of architectural definition for a royal burial, and eventually they deified him for his achievements. Archaeological investigation has shown that the first monument to cover the royal pit-burial was a mastaba, which was then enlarged by a bastion-like apron that rose up not quite as high as the original mastaba, thus creating a slight step from the apron to the top platform of the original mastaba. Perhaps inspired by this variation, further enlargements were made to

A six-stepped pyramid dominates the burial complex of King Zoser at Saqqara, Egypt. The pyramid, seen at right, is basically a greatly enlarged mastaba (burial mound), and is the focus of a funerary "city" patterned after the king's own palace. A gate in the reconstructed enclosure wall leads to courtyards and labyrinthine passages.

achieve, in elevation, first a four-stepped pyramid and then the six-stepped structure now standing in Zoser's Complex.

The stepped pyramid resembles in form the ziggurats of Mesopotamia, but Imhotep's design is considerably earlier than the Sumerian ziggurats built during the Third Dynasty of Ur (2112-2006 B.C.). The only other peoples conceiving and building such monumental constructions at the time Imhotep was configuring Zoser's tomb were the preceramic inhabitants of Peru, about whom, most plausibly, the Egyptians knew absolutely nothing—and we know only slightly more.

The stepped pyramid is a central focus for a large compound of buildings and courtyards surrounded by a great wall rising 33 feet (10 meters) and embellished with regularly spaced bastions. The outer faces of the wall are broken by gates, only one of which is a real gate that allows entry to the inner confines. Surrounding the pyramid are ritual courtyards, palaces, and temples, some of which are "effigies" or dummies with false doors—some even carved in low

The remains of the pyramid at Meidum, in Lower Egypt, represent a disastrous ancient attempt to transform a stepped structure into a smooth-sided geometric form similar to the pyramids at Giza. The pyramid collapsed during the renovation, leaving the original core of the stepped pyramid surrounded by heaps of debris.

relief to look as if partially opened. The complex looks like a city surrounded by its wall, but once inside, the "normal" realities of a town are turned into representative substitutions where normal reality is not an invited, or required, function. As with the maze-like tunnels and burial pits beneath the pyramid, the complex evokes the qualities of a labyrinth where the differences between illusion and reality are designed to be disorienting for the uninitiated. The high quality of construction and craftsmanship and the artistry of the reliefs and paintings point to an aesthetic that found meaning and, indeed, took pleasure in, such manipulations of normal reality. It should not be implied that there was something to be feared or bizarre in the labyrinthine disorientations of Zoser's Complex. As with most pyramid traditions, it represents a manifestation, an artful "bringing into form," of things and ideas not manifest in normal, consensual reality. It would have been wrong and misleading, and ultimately perhaps more bizarre, if the Complex of Zoser had been built as a real town.

Another feature of the complex is the so-called Southern Tomb set into the south wall. It is suggested by some scholars that this is Zoser's second tomb (or an effigy of his second tomb) and follows an already established tradition of

The unusual shape of the so-called Bent Pyramid at Dahshur, downriver from Meidum, is the result of a change of heart on the part of its builders during the pyramid's construction. After the collapse of the pyramid at Meidum, the Dahshur pyramid's architects reduced its angle of elevation from the steep 54.5 degrees to a safer 43.5 degrees.

building two royal tombs, perhaps in recognition of the union of the two Egypts at the beginning of the First Dynasty under the pharaoh Menes or Narmer: Upper Egypt of the Nile River proper and Lower Egypt of the delta. One tomb actually was to have housed the body of the pharaoh, while the other would serve as a cenotaph or memorial. The fact is, however, that most of the burials marked by pyramids may have been cenotaphs, as no bodies have been found in the burial chambers built beneath and within the pyramid massings. Concerning the absence of bodies, however, the usual explanation is that ancient tomb robbers penetrated the pyramids and, in carrying away all the fabulously rich offerings, carried the body as well, or sufficiently disturbed it so that it disintegrated without trace. Thus, another reason given for building two royal burials is that of making the grave robber's job more difficult, supposing, in this case, that no one would know or reveal which burial actually contained the body and the richest offerings. Seneferu, the first pharaoh of the Fourth Dynasty, however, seems to have gone one better and had three pyramids built.

The first known attempt to create a geometric, crystalline shape is at Meidum. Under Seneferu's patronage, a huge stepped pyramid rising in eight

The Great Pyramid of Khufu (Cheops) at Giza, outside Cairo, staggers the imagination and has inspired humans for many centuries. The sheer size of the pyramid—which stands some 481 feet (146.6 meters) high and whose base measures some 756 feet (230 meters) on each side—and the length of time required to build it hint at the builders' desire for a memorial that would last for eternity.

stages was planned and built; later, the steps were "filled-in" to create the smooth, planar sides—the first geometric pyramid. As Kurt Mendelssohn has deduced in his remarkable study, *The Riddle of the Pyramids*, the Meidum experiment was a disaster. The angled rise of the original, stepped pyramid was not engineered to achieve the desired or necessary angle of rise—52 degrees—or to support the additional weight of the packing stones that filled the spaces between the steps and the final facings of the geometric form. The pyramid collapsed. What can be seen today are the inner cores of the original stepped pyramid surrounded by the collapsed debris.

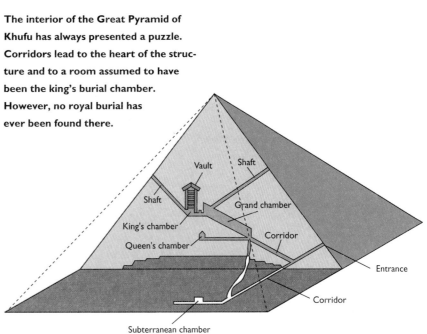

The interior of the **Great Pyramid** of **Khufu** has always presented a puzzle. Corridors lead to the heart of the structure and to a room assumed to have been the king's burial chamber. However, no royal burial has ever been found there.

While the Meidum pyramid was being renovated from stepped to geometric, Seneferu was building another pyramid downriver at Dahshur. Its construction was well along when the Meidum disaster occurred, and Mendelssohn suggests that this accounts for the very visible and awkward shift in its angle of elevation (54.5 degrees) to a more conservative one of 43.5 degrees—thus giving rise to its name, the Bent Pyramid. Seneferu tried again at Dahshur, this time succeeding in erecting a purely geometrically shaped pyramid, now known as the northern or Red Pyramid, but anciently called—more poetically—"Seneferu gleams." Understandably, it maintains the conservative and somewhat squat angle of elevation of 43.5 degrees.

Seneferu's son and successor, Khufu (or popularly, Cheops), caused the building of the Great Pyramid on the Giza plateau on the west side of the Nile River, just outside Cairo. It stands today because extraordinary engineering skills and invention were successfully brought to bear on achieving equally extraordinary aspirations for conception and design. From the time it was built, the Great Pyramid has aroused and inspired human imagination.

The core of the Great Pyramid was constructed by the careful piling up of some 2,300,000 blocks of local limestone, each weighing on the average two and one-half tons, thus creating a mass of 5,750,000 tons—and this figure does not include the harder limestone sheathing that once gave the pyramid its smooth-sided finish. Its four sides, each measuring, within inches, 756 feet (230 meters), rise in elevation at an angle of 52 degrees from the ground and meet at the apex 481 feet (146.6 meters) above the Giza

This reconstructed wooden bark, found dismantled in a pit near the southeastern corner of the Pyramid of Khufu, was undoubtedly used during the funeral of the pharaoh. Boat burials reflect the association of the pyramid with its River Temple, and may have been provided for the pharaoh's journey through the afterlife. The burials also point to the pervasive roles the Nile River played in the lives and imaginations of the ancient Egyptians.

plateau. The base of the pyramid covers over 13 acres (5.26 hectares). Just the recitation of its volumes, massings, weights, and measurements is enough to stun the mind. However, there are also the considerations of the more functional issues of tomb construction as well as the more conceptual issues involved in what all this ancient energy and activity may have meant in terms of economics, religion, politics, or philosophy.

The Great Pyramid's square plan is oriented with remarkable precision to the cardinal directions, and in reifying celestial and solar movements, it follows most pyramid-building traditions. While the four sides of the Egyptian pyramid are identical in their elevations, and thus no visual preference is marked for any of the cardinal directions (as is the case for the Mesoamerican pyramids where stairs mark their preferred side), the construction of the interior tomb does show a preference for the north. The entrance to the interior passageways leading to the tomb, called the descending corridor, is on the north side. In the Great Pyramid, this entrance was originally hidden behind the facing blocks of the hard Tura limestone. The angle of this ramp is 26 degrees and would point to the stars of the northern polar node. Today, because of the precession of the equinoxes, the actual node is marked by Polaris, or the North Star, but when the Great Pyramid was built, no star marked this point. Nonetheless, the stars closest to the then unmarked node revolved around it, tracing complete circles in the night sky. They neither rose nor set behind a horizon and were called the Indestructibles by the ancient Egyptians.

A ramp descending from the north side of the pyramid toward the burial chambers is a common feature for most pyramids built after Zoser's stepped pyramid, whether they are stepped or geometric, monumental or modest. The ramp is taken to literally point the way to immortality, to the place in the northern heavens where birth and death—rising and setting—are not the natural way of things.

Almost always, the actual burial chamber was centered, more or less, within and at the base of the pyramid or was excavated into the earth below. Thus, the placement of Khufu's tomb up within the hearting of the Great Pyramid is unique and, given the actual rooms and passageways known to lie within and below the pyramid, it seems that minds were changed during the construction as to where the actual chamber should be located. With all the astronomical knowledge needed to orient the pyramid properly and the engineering precision required to build it, this seeming indecision on the part of the architects, or perhaps Khufu himself, allows a glimpse of recognizable humanity behind the unimaginable monumentality achieved.

As with Zoser's Complex, Khufu's pyramid was part of a complex of structures built for religious purposes and for the perpetuation of the pharaoh cult. These structures are fairly standardized or predictable, consisting of the Valley or River Temple joined by a long, covered ramp to a Mortuary Temple, usually placed alongside the eastern face of the pyramid. The interior spaces of the temples and the enclosing walls of the ramp would be decorated with beautiful low reliefs and paintings, as well as hieroglyphic texts, the source of so much of our information about ancient Egyptian daily life and religious thought.

The Valley Temple was close to or within the region of arable land and often could be approached by river or canal, suggesting an importance given to water in the attendant rituals of burial and their perpetuation as a death cult. This may be borne out by the fact that boats were an important feature of the burial furniture, which during the Old Kingdom seems to have been reserved only for royal burials. The full-sized boats buried in boat-pits around the pyramid of Khufu could easily have navigated the Nile—indeed may have—before they were ritually buried. Called solar barks by some scholars, the boats may have symbolized the union of the royal person with the sun as it sailed across the sky.

It is not clear who within the ancient population had access to the temple complex associated with pyramids—certainly the priests and retainers of the pharaoh cults. In terms of design, scale, and decoration, however, the temples and the ramps would allow human use, and even human pleasure, while the pyramid would not, smooth-sided and closed as it was. A very real distinction was made between the monument rising improbably out of the desert and its surrounding temples which, by contrast, were horizontally oriented and designed to orchestrate the experience (probably one of religious initiation) of arriving at the Valley Temple and walking from the arable lands of normal life to the Mortuary Temple in the dry and desiccated desert, always under the looming presence of the pyramid.

ANCIENT SUMERIA

The lands between the Tigris and Euphrates rivers were also a place of great human genius, a genius quite different from the ancient Egyptian and usually explained by citing the very different conditions caused by a very different environment. Where the lands of Egypt are clearly defined by the Nile River and its narrow, arable valley, the flow and coursings of the Mesopotamian rivers were—and are not—as predictable, and no clear borders mark the lands through which they flow. Like the Nile, the Tigris and Euphrates flood annually, but unlike the Nile, their flooding time occurs during the rainy season, and the floods often become raging torrents, destroying as much as or more than is given back by the fertile muck and silt left behind. The ancient lands and peoples of Sumeria and Egypt are often described by using such ecological comparisons as just outlined in order to explain the many differences and the remarkably few similarities between the two civilizations as can be found in the archaeological records. The differences are otherwise difficult to understand, because ancient Egypt and Sumeria are both very early but contemporary civilizations developing in relative proximity to each other.

Furthermore, the region between the Tigris and Euphrates has little available stone, so building was done mostly with adobes. As there were even fewer trees, either for construction or for fuel, adobes were for the most part sun-dried—not baked—a building material that required constant maintenance. These facts account for the development over time of tells or mounds that now visibly mark the existence of an ancient town. Every generation or so, normal building maintenance would no longer suffice, and walls would be pushed over and built anew. Over time, a town would actually rise in elevation. Early Sumerian temples and palaces, faced with the more permanent kiln-baked bricks or rare limestone and, thus, more durable, could eventually find their town rising above them.

Sumerian civilization, moreover, had a more varied political and cultural history than the ancient Egyptian and, according to archaeological signs, began earlier, with clear urban patterns and specialized architectural forms for religious ceremony evident in the fourth millennium B.C. at such sites as Al Ubiad

The Tigris and Euphrates rivers, which converge in southeastern Iraq to form immense marshes, gave life to the civilizations of Mesopotamia, including ancient Sumeria. The marshes have long been the home of the Marsh Arabs.

and Uruk (also called Warka) in the lower valleys of the Tigris and Euphrates. According to archaeological classification, these early times are "Proto-literate," and span the fourth millennium. Thus, the Sumerian period covers the third millennium until the fall of the Third Ur Dynasty in 2016 B.C. More popularly, the fourth and third millennia are commonly referred to as Sumerian.

In ancient Sumeria, temples and shrines were built and maintained within the town or city, and were not ostensibly associated with burials and their attendant rituals. Because of this, we have a much clearer picture of Sumerian urbanism and domestic architecture; as the shrines were excavated, the town was also revealed. Furthermore, Sumerian shrines were often designed as domestic "houses" for the deity to which they were dedicated, and included kitchens, living areas, and bedrooms. No formal distinctions existed between secular and religious buildings: such differences as there were had to do occasionally with size but, more often, with the quality of building material, decoration, and sculptures.

During the 1930s, British archaeologist Leonard Woolley undertook the reconstruction of the Ziggurat of Ur. The illustration at right, based on Woolley's partial reconstruction, shows three stairways converging at a covered gateway to provide access to the ziggurat's upper levels. The elevated temple at the top is thought to have been the focus of the structure.

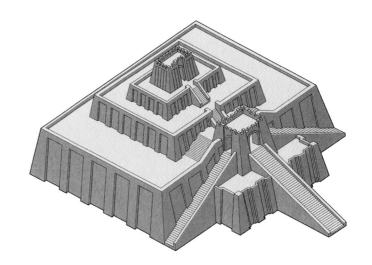

The partially reconstructed Ziggurat of Ur, shown at lower left in this aerial view, rises above the excavated outlines of the buildings that made up the sacred precinct of the great Sumerian city during the fourth millennium B.C. Only two of the ziggurat's original three terraces remain. The ziggurat, or "staged tower," was a feature of every Mesopotamian city. Unlike the Egyptian pyramid, however, the ziggurat was not a memorial to the dead, but rather a house or residence of the gods.

Another sign of religious function was a high platform on which the shrine was distinguished from its surrounding buildings. Platforms apparently were not necessary traits of religious function and, therefore, not used consistently; but the platform for the White Temple of Uruk (3500-3000 B.C.) is impressive and most likely the result of centuries of rebuilding. The platform visible today slopes inward as it rises some 40 feet (12 meters). It was faced with baked bricks, and its massive surfaces were supported by thin buttresses that create niches of shadow, relieving the oppressiveness of the platform surfaces. It is often pointed out that this massive construction predates anything of like kind in Egypt.

Because of its mass and rise, the White Temple platform is sometimes called a ziggurat, and many scholars, André Parrot in particular, believe the ziggurat as a distinct form of religious architecture has its origins in the ever-increasing size of the shrine or temple platforms. A formal distinction between platform and ziggurat, however, is not an easy one to determine, but generally, the ziggurat is considered to have been clearly defined and distinguishable from platforms only under Urnammu, the first ruler of the Third Ur Dynasty (2112-2016 B.C.). Often called a "staged tower," the ziggurat is usually square or squarish in plan and rises in elevation by successively smaller terraces set atop one another. The best preserved ziggurat was built by Urnammu at the city of Ur and was excavated in 1922 by Sir Leonard Woolley. The most famous ziggurat was constructed in Babylon by Nebuchadnezzar (604-562 B.C.) and described by Herodotus as rising in seven stages. Some have thought it to be the Biblical Tower of Babel. We know where this monument originally stood, and from the faint traces left today the stairways of the first stage were probably designed like the stairs of the much earlier Ziggurat of Ur.

The Ziggurat of Ur contains earlier structures, and therefore much of its mass was achieved by continuing architectural efforts beginning at least 500 years before Urnammu's reign. As reconstructed by Woolley from 1929 to 1939, it consisted of three terraces—only two remain today—supporting, ultimately, a temple or shrine some 65 feet (20 meters) above the ground. In elevation, the ziggurat could be (and has been) said to look like a stepped pyramid. But such a similarity is only possible through a verbal or written description of the shared formal units, the terraces or stages and steps. When looked at, even in photographs, the two types of monuments, the Egyptian stepped pyramid and the Sumerian ziggurat, look very different. Their visual impact seems to arise from very different conceptions about the monument's function and, more basically, from different aesthetics. Both the construction of the ziggurat and the conceptual framework that inspired it were quite different from its Egyptian relative. Basically, the Sumerian ziggurat achieved its height and mass by piling up successively smaller horizontal terraces, while the Egyptian stepped pyramid is a system of vertical buttresses of stepped heights leaning toward a central core.

The Ziggurat of Ur was designed as a place that focused toward the dramatic climax of the elevated temple. It was approachable, and its terraces were accommodating; it was meant to support religious ceremony and human engagement. A marvelous and dramatic system of stairs allowed access to terraces. Starting at the bottom of the outer sides of the mound, twin stairs rose diagonally up the face of the first stage to meet at the center and top, giving access to the first terrace. Perpendicular to these stairs and axially aligned to the mass of the ziggurat, another dramatic stairway rose on a ramp and joined the twin stairs at their meeting. This architectural event of joining was marked by a monumental, covered gateway. (This stairway design is thought to have been copied by Nebuchadnezzar for his ziggurat in Babylon some 1500 years later.) From this theatrical nexus, the way to the top was a single stairway continuing on the central axis to the second and third terraces and finally to the temple-shrine. (This last feature was totally absent when Woolley excavated, and while it is generally thought to be a proper and logical reconstruction, there is no actual evidence for its existence.)

A loose comparison may be made with the Egyptian pyramid. Both the ziggurat and the pyramid were anciently described as mountains, and this is a generalized similarity. Otherwise, the ziggurat and the pyramid were so differently conceived and designed as to make one wonder just how much importance should be given to the term mountain. The idea of mountain joins both the ziggurat and the pyramid to the larger group of pyramid traditions, but not so easily to one another.

The ziggurat, in common with most Sumerian urban and religious architecture, was situated so that its facades corresponded to the intercardinal points; thus, only the corners of the buildings would directly face north, south, east, or west. Why this was so may have to do with a greater interest in the northern and southern solstitial points of the solar year rather than with the equinoctial markings of east and west. It is a consistent orientation and certainly differs from the Egyptian alignments to the cardinal directions. In design, the Sumerian ziggurat was meant to evoke mountainous heights, and because of the stairs and temples supported by the "mountain," humans could actually approach the lofty domain of the gods. Unlike the ziggurat, the Egyptian pyramid could only suggest the connection between human and god by metaphor and conception, but not in reality, as the pyramid's design could not support human movement or interaction. These formal differences are related to functional ones: the ziggurat supported a high temple, while the pyramid was a marker, a memorial for a royal burial. The ziggurat supported the place where living humankind communicated or conjoined in a kind of marriage with the deity, or where the deity could descend from the heavens into the material world. The pyramid marked the place of burial and metaphorically formed the passageway for the dead soul to ascend to the gods.

The Great Stupa at Sanchi is the largest of three such structures at the central Indian site. Around the dome-shaped stupa stand four richly carved gateways, or *toranas*. These gateways mark the cardinal points: here we see the eastern torana. The gateways allow pilgrims to pass through the railing, or *vedika*, that surrounds the stupa itself. Pilgrims then walk clockwise around the structure.

ANCIENT INDIA

The stupas of India may not formally be obvious candidates for the idea of pyramid that is being developed in this book because their shape is dome-like and they seldom are monumental in size. They are an architecture of mass and have been described anciently as world-mountains, however, and so they are included. Furthermore, some scholars describe them as the Asian equivalents of the pyramids and ziggurats of Africa and the Near East and believe they may, in fact, derive some of their functional meaning from these ancient forms.

The conceptual origin for the stupa as world-mountain reaches far back into the prehistory of the subcontinent, while the first remaining architectural forms expressing this concept are no earlier than the third century B.C. when Buddhism became a state religion under the great Maurya Emperor, Aśoka (circa 274-237 B.C.). By this time, there is already a precision to the stupa's plans, and its various component forms are eminently developed to represent the body and life of Buddha. Unfortunately, given India's turbulent history, a place conquered and ruled by many different peoples— Dravidian, Aryan, Hindu, Buddhist, Persian, Greek, and Muslim—very few of the early stupas still stand. And as with much of Asian architecture, most of these have been consistently rebuilt, restored, and variously preserved.

Two things ought to be mentioned before giving an exemplary description of the stupa's form. The first is that the religious meanings of its forms are understood, not imagined, as is the case with regard to the more ancient Near Eastern monuments. And because of this, most discussions about stupas take on an intriguingly poetic, sometimes passionate, tone, by both European and Indian scholars. The second is the fact that the stupa, like most Indian architecture, exists as an armature for luxurious amounts of relief-carved imagery—didactic illustrations of the life and legends of Buddha. Thus, it is this imagery and its iconography that receives the most attention and, indeed, is most often reproduced photographically, so that the monuments are illustrated by details that focus on the images, rather than the whole structure. An informative exception is a little work entitled *Some Aspects of Stupa Symbolism*, by Anagarika B. Govinda, which outlines the formal proportions and meanings of the stupa and its component forms, albeit in reverent tones.

Stupa I of Sanchi was first built in the third century B.C. during the Mauryan Period, perhaps under the Emperor Aśoka. However, it has been enlarged and rebuilt many times, and the form, and especially the sculptural reliefs carved on its gates *(toranas)*, date from the first century A.D. Built to house relics of Buddha, the Stupa of Sanchi was constructed from compact rubble faced with brick, stone slabs, and stucco. The great dome *(anda)* is supported by a circular base *(medhi)*. (Bases can also be square in plan.) Atop the dome is a square balcony *(harmika)* from which rises the spire-like mast *(yasti)* supporting discs of decreasing size as they approach the top of the mast. The discs are called umbrellas *(chattras)* and recall the shading umbrellas held over rulers and potentates. The dome on its base is surrounded by a fence or railing *(vedika)* broken by four gates. Between the railing and the base of the stupa, there is an important space left for the clockwise circumambulation of pilgrims *(pradaksiná*, a sun-wise turn that keeps the right shoulder to the wall of the base).

Stupas are thought to be formally derived from ancient burial mounds that were shaped like simple round huts. The explicit connection between hut and burial mound is the maintenance of the ordinary necessities of life—shelter, food, clothing—in the burial. This seems to be so common a rationale for the form and decoration of tombs throughout the history of humankind as to omit the need for any further discussion. However, echoes of the ancient burial mounds are also evident in the construction of small shrines today; one might call them folk shrines. Heinrich Zimmer illustrates such shrines in his monumental work, *The Art of Indian Asia*. Shaped like small domes or vessels with constricted necks, the shrines have sticks with small flags rising from their tops or necks reminiscent of the masts and umbrellas of the stupa. They also seem to evoke the piles of sand that marked the predynastic pit-burials of Egypt—potent ephemera of human hopes. Whatever the history and meaning of the mound may be, by the time it is translated into the stupa, it is no longer an actual burial but a monument for housing relics—specifically the relics of Buddha—or, as they have been referred to, seeds *(bya)*. The forms and proportions have taken on specific meanings, wherein the body of Buddha is symbolized as the universe and is known metaphorically as Cakravartin, the world-ruler.

The major and massive feature of the stupa, the hemispherical dome, took its shape from ancient folk forms, the mounded shrine or simple hut. Metaphorically, it is the dome of the sky and probably ought to be understood as something shifting and ephemeral, because it is also referred to as an egg or a water bubble. It symbolizes the conditions for enlightenment. Anagarika Govinda tells of old stupas covered from top to base with small triangular recesses for lamps, "...so that the whole monument could be illuminated...as one huge radiating dome of light." The supernal balcony is the only outward manifestation of the holy mountain—the hub of the earth, Mount Meru—enclosed within the dome of the sky. (One has to imagine a pyramid within the hemisphere.) The harmika is where the relics are placed, above the world and beyond life and death. The mast rising from it represents the world axis—the tree of divine knowledge and life with its roots in primordial waters and its branches in the heavens. It is the backbone of the universe. The mast supports the royal umbrellas, the ultimate heavens of the gods. The fence separates the sacred from the profane and marks the place of procession. Entrance to this place is through gates oriented to the cardinal directions. At Stupa 1 of Sanchi, the gates are offset and designed to make the plan of the structure look like a swastika.

Indeed, a consistent feature of stupas is that their plans look like mandalas: symmetrically nested squares and circles. The best example of this, and perhaps the best preserved stupa, is the amazingly beautiful and complex structure built in the very center of the island of Java, at Borobodur. Constructed in the eighth century A.D., Borobodur manifests in very concrete ways all the metaphoric meanings of the stupa. The processional not only circumscribes the forms, but rises up through eight stages to the ultimate ninth. In performing the pradaksiná, the pilgrim passes around and up five square terraces within galleries whose walls illustrate the stories of Buddha and moral scenes proper to the level attained in the procession. The sixth, seventh, and eighth levels are circular and support 72 Buddhas seated within bell-shaped, trellised stupas. The transition from square to circular is from the material world of narrated story and common morals to the esoterica of spirit and time. According to art historian Benjamin Rowland, the number 72 refers to the number of years it takes within the precession of the equinoxes to mark one degree. To reach the top of Borobodur is to achieve the level of enlightenment and final liberation.

The later stupas, such as Borobodur, are designed to physically engage pilgrims who walk its measured terraces and, in so doing, literally are shown the way to enlightenment. Some scholars see in this a direct relationship to the ancient Sumerian staged-tower or ziggurat. However, the solar orientation of its gates is equinoctial, not solstitial, and its profound embodiment of the holy mountain within the dome of the sky is pre-Buddhist and performs the function of marker and memorial, which is more clearly related to the Egyptian pyramid. These connections are drawn, not to suggest foreign origins for the stupa, but to point out that its formal history embraces two pyramidal traditions: the memorial and the dramatic stage.

ANCIENT CAMBODIA

The Stupa of Borobodur illustrates the important influence and extent of Indian architectural (and religious) forms throughout Indonesia and, indeed, China. In Cambodia, the famous site of Angkor Wat reflects in its forms Indian influences expressing for the most part older Vedic-Hindu religious philosophies. Nonetheless, by the time Angkor Wat was built in the 12th century A.D., these origins had been thoroughly incorporated into the local Khmer style that also reveals the importance of contacts with Chinese architecture—especially tomb architecture.

The central focus of Khmer ceremonial architecture is the temple, a manifestation of the same world-mountain, the ancient Indian Mount Meru that is enclosed within the Buddhist stupa. The Khmer temple, however, was also inspired by another traditional Indian building type, the tower or *síkhara*, and can be thought of as a synthesis of these two different, original types.

The early Khmer temple, Baksei Chamkrong, built in A.D. 947, is modest: a stepped platform of five square terraces supporting a single temple approached by four stairways axially centered on each of the four terraced facades. The temple, also square in plan, supports a towering roof, the síkhara. In terms of its forms, the simple Khmer temple is closest in appearance to the stepped platforms of the ancient Maya and may also embody certain traits of the staged towers of the Sumerian ziggurat, a perception reinforced by the fact that the Khmer temple-tower was considered the residence of the deity, the place where the god would come when descending to earth.

When composed into a ceremonial city, such as Angkor Wat, the temple-tower is repeated and extended within a plan that expresses the city as a microcosmic manifestation of the universe. A central tower is the focus and the vertical axis of the universe-city and can be approached by a horizontal, axial

In Hindu and Buddhist belief, Meru was the cosmic mountain standing like a pillar between heaven and Earth. This Thai Buddhist painting, shown in its entirety at left, depicts Meru and the ascending heavens of the gods. At right, a detail of the painting's lower half shows Meru surrounded by seven successive mountain ramparts and intervening oceans.

The stepped pyramid at Borobodur in Indonesia incorporates a natural hill, and is the world's largest Buddhist stupa. The structure is built in the shape of a mandala, a Buddhist symbol that incorporates a circle within a square. Borobodur's nine terraced levels carry pilgrims around and around the structure until they reach the top. Here, 72 small, bell-shaped stupas—each containing a seated statue of the Buddha—surround the large central dome, and represent the attainment of enlightenment.

path that intersects processional galleries. Within the central tower is a portrait of the Khmer king in the image of the Cakravartin, the world-ruler.

Angkor Wat was built in what is now an almost impenetrable rain forest. It is part of an enormous royal and ceremonial center with similar compounds—such as Angkor Thom and Prah Khan—artificial lakes, and a connecting system of canals. Angkor Wat, however, is one of the best-preserved compounds built by the high Khmer civilization, which flourished from the 9th to the 15th centuries. It is an "effigy city," or cosmic city, laid out in plan as a series of expanding rectangles that grow from a central square that surrounds the high, central temple-tower. The outermost rectangle is a surrounding moat. More than anything found in India, the idea of a walled city constructed to make manifest ideal cosmic structures seems to have resonance with Chinese tomb construction elaborated during the Zhou and Q'in dynasties.

Clearly, to cross the surrounding moat and enter into the city of Angkor Wat is a ravishing, overwhelming experience. All who have written about it find it difficult to describe the city's vast scale and its unified but complex beauty. The moat itself is over 2.5 miles (4 kilometers) in circumference, and represents the cosmic ocean surrounding the world. After crossing the moat, the pilgrim continues along the causeway, which is the horizontal axis of the sanctuary, and encounters the first enclosing wall. In passing through its gate, the pilgrim symbolically crosses the mountain range that encircles the earth. As the pilgrim proceeds along the causeway, he or she passes through more gates into increasingly smaller rectangular spaces framed first by walls, then by corbel-vaulted galleries until the massive pyramid terrace that supports the central tower is reached. Here the emphasis changes from horizontal definition to a vertical one. The core of Angkor Wat, the five temple-towers, is supported on a square, stepped platform framed and quartered by galleries connecting the five tower-bases. The central tower, rising over 200 feet (61 meters) in height, is reflected by four others placed at the corners of the stepped platform and supported by smaller stepped pyramids abutting the main platform. In plan these look like bastions added to the central square. The towers housed statues of deities, and the central tower held the image of the god Vishnu conflated with the portrait of the Khmer ruler and patron of Angkor Wat, King Suryavarman II (A.D. 1112-1152). Suryavarman is shown to be a god-king, or Devaraja. (This is similar to the title of Cakravartin, or world-ruler, given to Buddha and exemplified by the form of the stupa.)

The many temples built in the royal ceremonial center of which Angkor Wat is a part are all oriented to the east. Angkor Wat alone is oriented to the west, and, because of this, is thought to have functioned in part as a mausoleum for its patron, King Suryavarman II. While stone coffins have been found under the central tower of several Khmer temples, none were found at

The five central towers of Angkor Wat represent the peaks of Mount Meru, the sacred mountain of both Hindu and Buddhist cosmology. The towers stand on a stepped platform surrounded by a wall. Only the Khmer king and his priests could ascend the two steep stairways to the central tower complex. The sandstone-faced towers were constructed during the 12th century A.D.

Angkor Wat. However, below the central tower is a deep well descending for 120 feet (36.5 meters), suggestive of the *axis mundi* or world pivot.

Other convincing evidence that the sanctuary was conceived as a mausoleum can be found in the first rectangular gallery, whose entire length is more than half a mile (804 meters) in circumference. Within its corbeled confines, a long (and perhaps the longest) continuous narrative, carved in relief, depicts the many stories of Vishnu/Suryavarman. To follow the stories in proper order, one must turn right and walk counterclockwise—that is, in the opposite direction of the pilgrim's way around the stupa. The most extraordinary scene depicts the Churning of the Sea of Milk, a story from

One of Angkor Wat's greatest treasures is the long bas-relief known as the Churning of the Sea of Milk, which depicts the Hindu creation myth of the "battle" between the gods and demons to release the elixir of life. In the detail shown at right, large and small demons clutch one end of the serpent Vasuki, the other end of which is held by the celestial gods under Hanuman, the Monkey God.

primordial times telling how the gods and demons cooperated to release the elixir of life from the cosmic seas. The giant serpent, Vasuki, is wrapped around the central mountain axis, and is pulled first in one direction by the gods, then in another by the demons, to churn up the sea and release the elixir. Vishnu sits atop the mountain in the center of the composition.

The conceptional daring behind such a scene is matched everywhere else within the sanctuary. Built of laterite and faced with sandstone, the whole is constructed by mortarless, drywall techniques. Major architectural forms, such as eaves, doors, tympana, cornices, and windows, are outlined by repeating "nested" frames, each cut at slightly different levels and each fashioned by different but harmonious shapes and designs. The effects are dazzling, visually confusing, and stimulating—an overwhelming lushness of form and shape.

ANCIENT CHINA

The architecture of China is for the most part an architecture of wood, and one that seldom aspires to the physical monumentality that we associate with the pyramids of ancient Peru, Egypt, and Sumeria. However, from at least the third century B.C.—that is, from the Q'in Dynasty through the following Han to Tang dynasties—great tombs, marked by pyramidal mounds, were constructed for the emperor and for wealthy feudal lords. But the greatest amount of archaeological attention has been focused on the burial pits that are associated with the tombs. The pits contain extraordinary ceramic sculptures crafted to represent, and to take the place of, the royal retinue and

armies maintained in life. Little archaeological work, however, has actually been carried out on the burial mounds themselves.

During the preceding Shang and Zhou dynasties, members of the elite classes were buried in subterranean pits. Using as an example the recently excavated Late Shang burial of Fu Hao (Tomb 5) at Yinxu in Henan Province, we know the pits were carefully constructed to preserve not only the body, but also the many extraordinary and beautiful works of art included in the burial. Fu Hao's tomb, rich as it was, was only visibly marked by a small shrine. Fu Hao's tomb is used, because she is always described as a consort or concubine of King Wu Ding, and certainly there is no reason to doubt this. However, inscriptions on bronzes and other articles of her tomb reveal that she was also a brilliant military strategist who achieved the rank of general and led many successful campaigns for King Wu Ding. She probably was ruthless as well. Like many elite tombs of this period, her burial rituals included human sacrifices. It is thought that the beautiful works of art found in the burial pits of later tombs were, indeed, substitutes for the actualities of the Shang sacrificial practices—following the dictates of Confucius against such barbarity.

During the Later (or Eastern) Zhou Dynasty, tumuli, or mounds supporting ceremonial halls, were constructed over burials. A reconstruction of the Zhongshan Mausoleum (or funerary park) in Hebei Province, made from an ancient bronze plaque showing it in plan, is illustrated in art historian Wu Hung's article, "From Temple to Tomb." Dr. Wu explains the shift from temple to tomb as the result of a new type of ritual that centered in individuals rising in power during the breakup of the Zhou Dynasty rather than on the family lineages that claimed the worshipper's attention at the time Fu Hao's tomb was built.

In 1974, farmers digging a well east of the Lishan burial mound discovered a number of life-size terra-cotta figures. Excavation of the site by Chinese archaeologists revealed an extraordinary ceramic army buried in three wooden-roofed pits near the tomb of the First Emperor. Shown here are a group of the restored ceramic figures from Pit No. 1, placed in their original positions.

A double wall surrounds the reconstructed Zhongshan Mausoleum, which shares many formal features with the complex of Angkor Wat. The plan is a series of repeating and nested rectangles and squares cut through by a central axial pathway. Within the walls, five stepped pyramids are supported by a raised platform. The central, axial one marks the tomb of the king; the other four, apparently, marking those of his consorts. The height of the tomb mound would symbolize the rank of the individual. While rank was supposedly achieved through personal accomplishment, such accomplishments apparently could be self-determined, depending in large part on personal ambition and economic abilities. Wu Hung cites a contemporary text, *Lushi chungiu*, written at the end of the Eastern Zhou Dynasty:

> Nowadays when people make burials, they erect tumuli tall and huge as mountains and plant trees dense and luxuriant as forests...Their cemeteries are like towns and cities! This may be a way of making a display of their wealth to the world, but how could they serve the deceased [with such extravagance]!

The ceramic figures unearthed at Lishan include infantry, archers, charioteers, and cavalry. The troops represent the honor guard that would have been stationed outside the imperial capital of Xi'an. Like this restored cavalryman, the figures are extraordinarily realistic, and show individual variations of stance, facial expression, and hairstyle.

The First Emperor of Q'in, who ruled from 220-210 B.C., unified China for the first time in that country's history, and his ambition and "rank" were both phenomenal. He had built the Great Wall of China to protect his northern borders, and he also had built an extraordinary funerary park at Lishan, about 15 miles (24 kilometers) east of Xi'an (Sian) in Shensi Province. The funerary park and mausoleum of the First Emperor, Chih-huang-ti (who died in 210 B.C.), was rectangular in plan and double-walled, like the Zhongshan Mausoleum, and oriented to the north and south. However, only one tumulus was built within the inner wall. Both the walls and the tumulus were made of tamped or pounded earth. The tumulus, in fact, may have been made by adding pounded earth to a natural hill. Because the building material is pounded earth, the measurements of the walls and the tumulus are approximate: the perimeter of the outer wall measured well over 3 miles (4.8 kilometers). The walls were not very tall—about a yard (one meter) in height—but they were 19 to 23 feet (6 to 7 meters) wide. Were they processionals?

The tumulus measures 1148 feet by 1132 feet (350 meters by 345 meters) and rises to an approximate height of 130 feet (39 meters), perhaps in two stages. (Robert Thorp, in his article, "An Archaeological Reconstruction of the Lishan Necropolis," published an early photograph of the tumulus taken by Victor Segalen, probably in 1914. This clearly shows two stages, while modern photographs only show a rounded mound.) At the time of this writing, the tumulus has not been excavated. According to historical records (Sima Qian's *Historical Records*), whose statements in this regard are problematic, the mound covered an extensive underground construction, a deep pit reinforced with bronze plates against underground springs. The tomb was built as a royal palace with, of course, a great hoard of treasure. Supposedly, mercury was used to simulate seas and rivers that were then made to flow by mechanical means. Also, armed crossbows were set up in secret, strategic points and mechanically triggered to fire at unwary intruders.

All of this would seem the stuff of legend, except for what is contained in three pits found outside the east wall of the funerary park. These pits contained the justly famous life-size ceramic army—an honor guard comprising cavalry, infantry, archers, and chariots—representing guard troops that would have been stationed outside the city in actuality. Every member of Chih-huang-ti's honor guard and army is a remarkable work of art. Each warrior is rendered as an individual portrait with a unique physical appearance and personality—we can recognize the extrovert, the introvert, intelligence, rashness, existential concern, a confident nature. All this information is mirrored in the faces of the warriors; their bodies are like mannequins. However, each soldier is appropriately dressed according to his rank and station.

Through the sculptures of the burial pits at Lishan, we get a glimpse of the ideals and concepts that may have informed the building of the walled funerary park. The soldiers are not miniature, and one does not stand for many. Not only are natural scale and actual numbers duplicated, the individuality of the warriors who make up the numbers is duplicated—that is, they are not like toy soldiers made from the same mold. There is a one-to-one reproduction from the actual to the sculptural—no reductions, no schematization, ostensibly no conceptualization. If this is how an army is reproduced, then it seems possible to suppose that within the walls of the funerary park a real city with its temples, shrines, and gardens was built next to, and under, a mountain with everything reproduced in its proper and actual scale. Described as a megalomaniac, perhaps Chih-huang-ti did not wish his mountain to stand for the world-mountain at the center of the Earth, but for a specific, original mountain—his alone. It did not matter that, being his own tumulus, it was unique. Ipso facto, Chih's mountain was the center of the world.

Possibly the most easily recognized structure in the world, the Great Pyramid of Khufu surprises many who see it up close. It is constructed of built in three distinct phases. Two different types of limestone formed the interior structure, while a fine, white limestone (now stripped away)

3

HOW TO BUILD A MOUNTAIN

Pyramids are an architecture of mass. Constructed with little or no interior space, they resemble gigantic sculpture rather than architecture as the latter word is normally understood. Plan and elevation are the main architectural features that define the outline of the pyramid—the shape of its base and its overall silhouette. Three things, then, would concern the pyramid-builder: the siting and shaping of the base according to a plan; the raising of the mass according to a prescribed elevation;

more than two million limestone blocks, and was
was used as an outer sheathing.

and its final silhouette in the exterior shaping, or sculpturing, of the elevated mass. One note of caution is in order at this point, however. Our information about ancient construction techniques varies because of what has, and has not, been excavated by archaeologists. Even with the Egyptian pyramids of the Giza plateau, we are required to make analogies about their construction strategies with other less monumental pyramids. In addition, simply because of their sheer size, pyramids are formidable and expensive structures to excavate.

PLANS

Pyramids rise from square, rectangular, and circular plans, and these are carefully sited and oriented to express, in concrete form, solar and occasionally stellar events. The latter, however, have not been as thoroughly explored and tested. The work of archaeoastronomers such as Anthony Aveni has made orientation to stellar movements best known in Mesoamerica at the present time.

The mandala is a sacred image, a graphic form of the universe, used by Buddhists and Hindus during meditation. Its circle-within-a-square design is the basis of the design of the Buddhist stupa, an architectural version of the cosmos. In the plan of Indonesia's Stupa of Borobodur shown at right, the square base of the stupa rises in stages to the central dome, which represents the dome of heaven enclosing the world-mountain as it rises from Earth to heaven. The circle-within-the-square theme also can be seen in the painted Tibetan Vaicravana mandala shown on the opposite page.

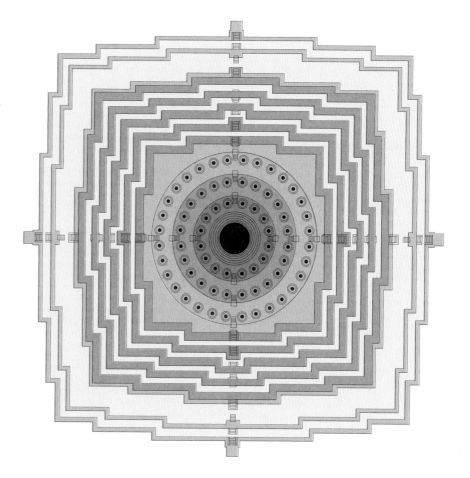

Square plans, with their equal sides, do not in themselves suggest any hierarchical direction. This must be provided by stairs, ramps, or other exterior designs. In plan, then, no one side of the square is favored over another. It is ecumenical in shape—that is, all four sides are the same—and chosen by pyramid builders everywhere. Only in Egypt, however, is this inherent ecumenical character allowed to inform the rise of the pyramid in elevation.

Even more equivocal than the square is the circular plan, which of course is continuous, offering no directional focus through its form. And like the square plan, if there is to be any focus, this must be provided by additional and exterior features. Of the traditions reviewed in the previous chapter, only Indian and Mesoamerican pyramid-builders chose the circular plan.

The square and circle are used as plans for the Buddhist stupa and the temple-towers in Khmer "cities". In plan, stupas often combine the square and circle in a purposeful recreation of a symmetrical mandala, a sacred image composed for meditation. And one should suppose that the elevations arising from such plans are manifestations of meditational states. Such an

PYRAMID STYLES

The various types of pyramids are most easily recognized by their profiles: battered, domed, or stepped.

The battered profile is characteristic of the ancient Egyptian pyramids, and describes the slope of its sides rising up and leaning inward from the base to meet at an apex. Egyptian pyramids always rise from a square plan or base, and in their elevations of four battered profiles they form the abstract shape of a tetrahedron. The Egyptian elevation was also monumentally plain, in that it did not support any other architectural or decorative features.

The domed profile is curved and provides the characteristic shape of the ancient Buddhist stupa. Like the Egyptian battered profile, the stupa's elevation and profile stress an abstract geometric shape, in this case, the sphere. However, unlike the Egyptian pyramid, the dome of the stupa was not left plain, but was embellished with meaningful ornamentation at the apex of its curve and in the processional paths ranging around its curved sides. The domed profile must rise from a circular base, but in plan, and indeed as a meaningful tradition in building stupas, it often appears that the domed elevation rises from a square base, reflecting the circle in the square used to compose the sacred image of the mandala.

The stepped profile alternates its rising, which can be battered or vertical, with a horizontal step or stage, and creates a stepped-back elevation. It is the most variable pyramid style because its diagnostic profile need not be compromised by differences in proportion between rise and step or by the various kinds of decorations that may be added to its forms. Furthermore, it can variously rise from square, circular, or rectangular plans. The stepped pyramid was the most common kind, and was built in ancient Egypt, Sumeria, India, and Cambodia, as well as in the ancient Americas, where it was the primary form for monumental architecture.

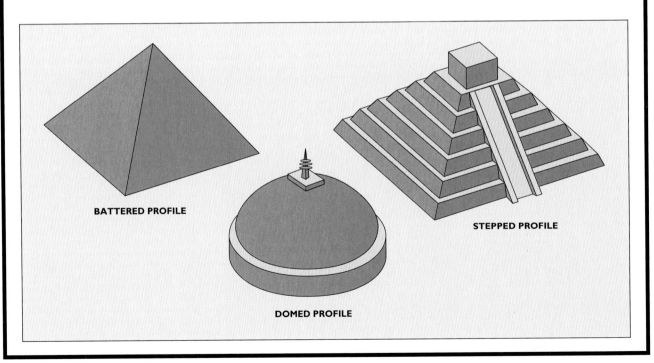

BATTERED PROFILE

DOMED PROFILE

STEPPED PROFILE

idea is clearly expressed at Borobodur. The galleries and temple-towers of Angkor Wat may have been similarly conceived, but this is not as evident from their forms. Here, a square plan is centered within and combined with rectangular plans that reflect or refer to it but do not repeat it. The central square is crossed by galleries that mark the cardinal directions. In plan, the square looks like a mandala, but as it expands into the rectangles of the Angkor Wat complex , it takes on a more intellectual (less meditative) design.

The effigy volcano of La Venta needs to be mentioned at this time. Its plan is thought to be a fluted circle that in elevation would resemble a volcano. There is little question that it could be classed as a circular plan, but its status as an effigy comes from being a more realistic rendition of a mountain than most other pyramids whose forms "stand for" mountains but do not mimic such natural features as valleys. Because of this, its sculptural nature is more prominent than usual and leads to its possible connection to, or inspiration for, the effigy mounds of North America found within the vast Mississippi basin, such as the famous Serpent Mound near Chillicothe, Ohio. The North American mounds have been, somewhat arbitrarily, left out of the review of the previous chapter, because it is uncertain that they functioned as metaphoric mountains. The La Venta pyramid may be unique in this realism but, as discussed in Chapter 2, there are strong suggestions that the tumulus constructed over the First Emperor's tomb at Lishan was also conceived as a realistic mountain. Furthermore, sculptures directly associated with both the Chinese and the Olmec mountains evoke similar questions about scale and reality.

Rectangular plans, like squares, are common choices in all places except Egypt. The rectangle is more dynamic than the square or the circle, and can illustrate a directional focus signaled by the differences between the long and short sides. It also allows greater flexibility in directional siting, because the proportions between the long and short sides of the rectangle can be adjusted to reflect, or point toward, two different celestial events that are not structurally related to each other. That is to say, the rectangular plan could be oriented to the cardinal directions, the long sides oriented east/west. Given a proportional difference between the length of the long sides to the short (north/south) sides, the angled corners would point toward different directions, such as the solstitial points on the horizon. Thus, the pyramid could reflect points relating both to the equinox and the solstice, as well as the cardinal directions.

The question of how the ancient architects were able to achieve accuracy in their geometric plans of the square, the circle, and the rectangle is one that is raised fairly often. Archaeology seldom allows for direct knowledge of this unless the geometer's tools have been found or contemporary documents tell of such methods. For the more ancient pyramids, modern students must adduce such abilities.

In contrast to Egyptian pyramids, those of Mesoamerica were built from point-to-point observation, an activity being engaged in here by a modern-Governor was built at Uxmal, Mexico, about A.D. 900, an observer in a doorway could have scanned across the top of a distant pyramid and seen

With the Egyptian pyramids, there remain many questions about the ancient knowledge of geometry, especially knowledge about the ratio of the circumference of a circle to its diameter, or pi (3.141). One-half this ratio, or $^1/_2$ pi, is the ratio of height to circumference in the pyramids of Giza, and as Kurt Mendelssohn says, this is "an accuracy that cannot comfortably be dismissed as fortuitous...." Such a ratio results in, or is the result of, the angle of elevation, 51 degrees 52 minutes, and the consistency with which Egyptian pyramids were raised at this precise angle shows it to have been a conscious decision. However, it is one that is on the edge of practicality, because steeper angles could compromise the structural validity of the mass.

In the myriad efforts to reconstruct the means and the methods by which the ancient Egyptian engineers and architects constructed their great edifices, Mendelssohn's explanation of the consistent ratio of $^1/_2$ pi and the resultant angle of elevation is the most convincing to this author. (Mendelssohn credits an engineering colleague, T.E. Connolly, for his insights.) The height of the pyramid was figured in royal cubits; that is, the span between elbow and middle finger standardized as 20 inches (50.8 centimeters) in the Old Kingdom. But in order to reach a desired height, the horizontal measurements of the plan and the angle of elevation had to be precisely figured. On the ground, a measuring rope could stretch and was therefore not an accurate means for making precise measurements of long distances. Instead, Mendelssohn suggests that a wooden drum was constructed to be one royal cubit in diameter. One revolution of the drum would be a "rolled cubit," and one had only to count the number of revolutions to achieve an accurate measurement. The relationship between the diameter of the wooden drum, one cubit, and its circumference, a rolled cubit, would produce the $^1/_2$ pi ratio whether the ancient Egyptians were knowledgeable of such a geometric constant or not. (This explanation is more elegant, in the mathematical sense, than the mystical and esoteric explanations that go on to show how the ancient Egyptians knew the circumference of the Earth and its precise distance from the Moon.)

The ancient Mesoamericans, as exemplified by Maya architectural achievements, were berated by the British archaeologist J. Eric S. Thompson for their failure to create right angles. As he had observed, when measured for accuracy, the angles of the bases (that is, the angles of the plans) of pyramids were seldom if ever true right angles. Thompson's implication, here, is that such measurements were not possible, because the Maya lacked any knowledge of geometry and they "eye-balled" their plans and elevations, building out of traditional experience—folk architecture—rather than from preconceived plans.

In the last 15 years or so, this characterization of Maya architecture has changed, not because Thompson's observation was incorrect, but because he measured the wrong thing. The ancient Mesoamericans used point-to-

day archaeoastronomer. When the House of the Venus rise as the morning star.

point lines of observation. One stood in doorways, or on the center of stairs, and looked toward doorways or stairs of other structures or at natural or human-made features (gnomons) in the landscape or on the horizon. Many of these supposed lines of sight have been carefully measured and, as shown by architect Horst Hartung at Palenque, Tikal, and Uxmal, the ancient lines of sight were related to one another by a very accurate geometry—but it is a "geometry of the void" expressed or manifested only when used by participants: someone must stand at a particular place and look in a certain direction in order to participate in the geometrical precisions and the ideas expressed through it. It is not implicit in the masses and forms of the architecture, but rather in the exterior designs of doors and stairs. Thus, the major alignments of Mesoamerican pyramids are taken from points on the stairways or from the temple doors; the sighting of the zenith sun setting from the center of the western stairs of the Pyramid of the Sun at Teotihuacán being a prime example.

The precise location of pyramids and the way their plans were oriented seems to have been sensitive to several factors: whether the site was situated within a city or without; whether it incorporated a natural hill or other natural feature within its form; and what events, usually celestial, its orientation should reflect. The first condition, inside or outside the city, divides pyramid traditions into two general groups: pyramids that were conceived as part of the civic space and pyramids that were conceived as outside civic concerns. This grouping will be discussed in more detail in Chapter 5, but in general, the pyramids built outside the cities were primarily memorials, markers for burials, often part of a necropolis. Pyramids inside the town functioned as temples and were the focus for civic and/or religious ceremony.

Many pyramids are known to, or else are thought to, incorporate natural features within their masses. Often, knowledge of this stems from legend rather than archaeology, such as the lake and mountain Herodotus mentions when he describes the interior of the Great Pyramid of Khufu. Nonetheless, many scholars mention the possibility that the Great Pyramid incorporates a hill of natural bedrock within its mass. This has been suggested, as well, for the First Emperor's tumulus in Lishan. Of the pyramids mentioned in Chapter 2, it is known that the great Pyramid of the Sun at Teotihuacán was situated over a natural cave, and that the Pyramid of Inscriptions at Palenque incorporated a natural hill within its mass. Perhaps the temple-fortress of Sacsahuamán represents the most overt, or intense, expression of this siting feature wherein natural forms are integrated into the construction.

The siting of pyramids to reflect cosmological structures is a characteristic described for all pyramid traditions, but accurate measurements of these orientations are few. For most, their orientations have to do with the movements of the sun and, using what we do know, pyramids can variously reflect the sun in

The Toltec capital city and stronghold of Tula, north of modern-day Mexico City, now stands stripped of its splendor. As with most Mesoamerican pyramids, its builders used the rubble-fill building technique, stabilized by outer walls of roughly cut facing stones and smoothly finished with a white limestone plaster.

its equinoctial, solstitial, or zenith passages. To site the pyramids accurately, astronomical knowledge must be brought to bear in the planning through the ability to chart the cardinal directions.

True east and west can be located at the time of equinox, but a more precise means of calculating cardinal directions would come from tracing the arc of the sun as it travels from east to west (done with a gnomon casting a shadow as the sun moves through the day); that is, by drawing a straight line from the shadow point at sunrise to the shadow point at sunset and bisecting the line. A line drawn from the gnomon to the point of bisection points to true or polar north.

The only exception to the use of solar and stellar orientations has been postulated for the early pyramids of South America erected along the desert coast of Peru. Here, scholars have suggested that the irregular, but generally northeastern, orientations of ceremonial plans have to do with purely local circumstances—such as pointing toward the source of a valley river or toward a particular peak among the towering Andes Mountains—rather than cosmological ones.

INTERIOR MASSES AND ELEVATIONS

Once the plan is properly laid out, the impressive work of creating the bulk of the pyramid begins. The ancient builders used three ways to construct the mass of the pyramid: tamped-earth technique, piling up clay-like earth and stabilizing it by packing or tamping it down; rubble-fill technique, piling up a rubble mixture of dirt, clay, and stones and stabilizing it with facings of baked adobe or stone; or modular-fill technique, with preformed modules of cut stone, brick, or adobe, which in themselves provide stability, but are always "finished" on the exterior walls with carefully cut stones and/or smooth stucco. The method of bag-fill used within the very ancient Peruvian pyramidal platforms of Aspero is a unique type of modular-fill.

The tumulus and surrounding walls of the funerary "city" of the First Q'in Emperor at Lishan (circa 210 B.C.) were constructed with tamped earth, as was the effigy volcano of La Venta, which was raised some 400 years earlier (circa 600 B.C.). Given the natural, erosive effects of time and weather, one would not expect the tamped-earth technique to be particularly enduring, and most likely, many structures made by such a technique are now lost to us. Indeed, their sheer monumental scope is probably a major reason the effigy pyramid and the tumulus have been preserved.

On the other hand, because of the material and technique of tamped-earth construction, some landscape features thought to be natural hills may turn out to have been constructed ones. The descriptions of the First Emperor's tumulus suggest it had been planted with a "forest" of trees, and that the original desire was to make the mound appear as a natural feature. Certainly, the effigy volcano of La Venta could be so interpreted, except that it was raised in the improbable environment of coastal swamps. Tamped-earth constructions are made of the stuff of their place; they are consonant features that are distinguished as human-formed only through exaggeration or improbability.

Rubble-fill is a piling of a mixture of things—stones, clay, dirt, refuse from middens. (In this regard, I find myself thinking in terms of modern construction projects, such as golf courses, built on or around old landfills and euphemistically referred to as "waste management" projects.) Often, the exterior walls would be constructed first and then the fill laid or dumped in. Or a pile of coarse rubble would be massed, surrounded by a wall, and then finer fill would be added to completely fill the interior established by the wall. Either way, for massive projects such as pyramids, this procedure would be done in stages that matched the rising of stepped or terraced elevations. Not all stepped pyramids were constructed with rubble-fill (for example, the Sumerian ziggurats), but the use of such a massing technique works best in staged constructions.

The use of the rubble-fill technique is most characteristic of ancient Mesoamerican architectural projects, where almost all pyramids have been so constructed. The facing walls of stone, often only roughly dressed, were laid with mortar and covered with stucco to give a smooth finish. At Teotihuacán, the great Pyramid of the Sun may have had the bulk of its interior mass constructed of adobe brick. Adobes have been found in its heartings, but we do not know the extent of their use—they may have been the exterior architecture for a tomb, or the first massings, called the "hidden pyramid" by archaeologist R.E. Smith, underlying the whole structure. After the Pyramid of the Sun was built, work began in earnest for the next monumental project at that site, the Pyramid of the Moon, a rubble-filled structure that was raised in stages. The construction of the stabilizing walls was elaborated within the interior areas of each stage. Basically, lateral and cross-walls were constructed within each walled stage resulting in a grid of pockets that were then filled with rubble, increasing the structural viability of each stage. This became the usual means employed in Mesoamerica for containing the rubble-fill.

The use of rubble-fill, walled by cobbles and roughly dressed stones set in copious amounts of mortar, then covered with stucco for a smooth finish, is not the recipe for an architecture that will withstand "all time". Descriptive terms, such as "impractical" and "lack of concern," are used by today's critics, but these seem to echo the 19th-century European aesthetics of the French archaeologist Désiré Charnay when he refers to the architecture of Uxmal, Yucatán, as, "wanting in both accuracy and symmetry...materials are ill-cut...joints far apart...filled up with cement...there isn't a French bricklayer who couldn't do quite as well and better."

Implicit in such criticism is the assumption that monumental architecture, and especially pyramids, should aspire to millennial permanency. When this doesn't happen, as is the case with the rubble-filled pyramids of Mesoamerica, then it is regarded as a lack, and insufficiency of structure and form and, ultimately, of cultural will and stamina. A more generous, and probably a truer, interpretation would be that the monumental architecture of Mesoamerica was the result of a cultural aesthetic in which material and technique combined purposively to serve that aesthetic in a positive way. That is, one should understand this architecture as it is, rather than as it is not.

Another tradition that consistently uses rubble-fill is the one described for the Buddhist stupa. Earth, pebbles, and stones were compacted together and enclosed in a curved mantle of brick. This, in turn, could be faced with stone slabs and/or stucco. The construction technique is very similar to that of ancient Mesoamerica, but the resulting hemispherical form is quite different and generally not very grand in scale. The exception, of course, is the Stupa of Borobodur, but it is not known how its final mass was achieved.

Modular-fills are the most stable techniques for massing form. Fills of unbaked adobes are least permanent, while cut-stone is the most permanent. After the plan is laid out, the modules would be laid in horizontal courses designed to manifest, more or less roughly, the desired profile in elevation—stepped or battered. The final elevations would be finished by a different and more durable material. The pyramids of Peru (bag-fill and adobe-fill, faced with stone and stucco), Sumeria (adobe, faced with brick), and Cambodia (laterite, faced with sandstone) were built in this manner. And so were the pyramids of Egypt (limestone, faced with a harder limestone).

The construction of the modular-fills for Egyptian pyramids, however, has been looked at most closely and represents a clear expression of a desire for permanence. The coursing techniques used for the early stepped pyramids of the Third Dynasty and for the geometric shapes of the Fourth Dynasty are complex but solidly engineered designs that, essentially, expand outward from a central core rather than being built upward from the base. This may, in part, be the result of a cherished tradition that began with Imhotep's expansion of Zoser's mastaba into a stepped pyramid, wherein the central core, the mastaba, was built around by rising steps. Imhotep's constructional solution for his enlargements was to design each step like a surrounding buttress with its stones coursed at a diagonal leaning down and inward, perpendicular to the angled or battered profile of the step.

Diagonally sloping course work is the manner in which the inner pyramids of the first geometric shapes were constructed, in particular, Seneferu's Bent Pyramid at Dahshur. Each step would correspond to an encircling buttress of diagonally coursed stones around a central core.

Kurt Mendelssohn, who provides one of the best descriptions of how the Egyptian pyramids were built, supposes that the famous geometric pyramids of Giza were probably engineered in a similar manner. Once the inner, stepped pyramid was constructed, then packing stones would be laid to fill in the steps. These were laid, or coursed, horizontally and, as the packing stones rose up the sides of the pyramid, they created small steps (relatively small, given that the stones of the inner fill often weighed two tons) rising up the sides to the apex. The packing stones are what are seen today as the surface of the three great pyramids at Giza. Once the packing stones were in place, the mass of the pyramid would be sheathed with a harder stone, precisely cut to fit into the small steps and to achieve a smooth outer surface.

The architectural principle of the corbel involves the forming of a single stability by uniting two unstable units. The corbel springs from two vertical supports, with each course of bricks extending slightly beyond the one beneath it. When the two "slanting" walls meet each other, they form an arch of great strength and stability. Examples of this technique can be seen in the South Gate of the temple of Angkor Thom, Cambodia (*left*), and in the Arch of the Nunnery at Uxmal, Mexico (*right*). The small interior spaces of most pyramids were also constructed using the principle of the corbel.

Because of the value of the hard limestone facing, it has been removed—actually quarried—at various times for other building projects. When this began is unknown.

INTERIOR SPACES

When interior spaces, such as rooms and passageways, were located within the massing fills—not cut out of bedrock, as in pit burials—they were inevitably constructed using the principle of the corbel. This is true of the Egyptian, the Chinese, the Indian and Indonesian, the South American, and Mesoamerican pyramids—all traditions that placed small interior spaces within the pyramid. The corbeled arch and vault are based on the principle of forming a single stability by uniting two unstable units—two negatives thus making a positive. The corbel springs from a vertical support, a coursed wall, by extending each successively higher course slightly beyond the one below it. From one wall, this is an unstable construction, but when it meets a similar, but opposing, construction from a parallel wall, the two diagonally and outwardly sloping walls combine to form an arch of great stability.

Because of the way in which the corbeled arch and vault is designed and built, it does not permit generous interior openings, and when these spaces do occur, they are always small relative to the mass of the pyramid. The corbeled arch is also called the "false arch," and most commentators feel compelled to add a phrase such as "the builders were ignorant of the true arch...." Implicit in such terminology is the assumption that the "true," or Roman, arch is the most desirable form and, when attained, marks an evolutionary watershed in architectural knowledge and technology.

In an architecture of mass, however, the true arch would be a disastrous choice for opening up interior spaces. Its structural principles would collapse under the profound weight of the fill, whatever kind was used. Structurally, the corbel arch is the best solution. It properly distributes the weight by working with, not against, the gravity of the mass that presses down and out. The energies of massive weight split at the point of the corbel and move out along its sides. Use of the corbel was a structurally sound decision on the part of the ancient architects and engineers, and certainly not a sign of ignorance or primitive attainments.

There is another aspect of the corbel that might bear on its being the choice of pyramid-builders: its resultant form is pyramidal and, therefore, consonant with the structure in which it was being used. Nothing (that I know of) in the literature on pyramids speaks of this, but it is possible that it, too, played a role in the designs of the pyramid-builders: to open up a small pyramid of negative space within a monumental pyramid of mass.

EXTERIORS

The exteriors of pyramids are first defined, and perceived, by the profile of their elevations. Stairs and ramps can change the profile, and exteriors are further defined or refined by the enhancements and designs added to profile and stair.

The elevated profiles of pyramids are few in number and reflect the small number of plans from which they originate. The Egyptian pyramids present what has been thought of as the classic profile, here classed as battered, with leaning sides rising to a point. Like the battered Egyptian profile, the curved profile of the Buddhist stupa is unique to its cultural origins. The stepped profile, on the other hand, was employed by many peoples at many different times: Sumerians, Mesoamericans, Indonesians, and Chinese. It is the most common pyramidal profile, and, because of this, really ought to be considered the classic form of the pyramid.

Because the stepped profile has two elements—one horizontal (the terrace or step), and one vertical or battered (the stage)—it shows the greatest variation. Proportional relationships between step and stage can vary widely, and the elevation of the stage can vary from vertical to deeply battered, even

The stepped pyramid has two elements: the horizontal step and the vertical stage, or riser. A distinctive variation of this form, known as *talud-tablero*, was used at Teotihuacán when a box-shaped step was framed to enhance its outline. The talud-tablero profile can clearly be seen on the smaller pyramids that line the Street of the Dead, at Teotihuacán, and was a hallmark of that great city.

within one culture and time. At Teotihuacán, after the pyramids of the Sun and Moon were constructed, a particularly beautiful stepped form, the so-called *talud-tablero,* became the hallmark of that great city. The talud, a battered profile, much like the Egyptian pyramid, was articulated by tableros, box-shaped steps with a vertical profile that encircled the rising talud. The tablero would be slightly cantilevered out from the talud and framed. The effect of shadow and sun across the surfaces of the pyramid constructed with the units of talud and tablero is so striking it must have been the result of a conscious strategy employed by the architects who built the many pyramids that line the Street of the Dead.

Stairs and ramps give access to the top of the pyramid, and only the Egyptian pyramid and the early Indian stupas at Sanchi exclude them by design. They also were used to indicate or channel attention to the place or places of important focus and meaning. That is, the ramps and stairs would lead to a temple at the top of the pyramid and were centered upon one or more sides to emphasize the orientation (solar, stellar, or otherwise) of the monument.

The visual rhythms of the risers and steps of the stairways are in marked contrast to the rhythms of the stepped profiles of the pyramid, and a tension that is both visual and structural is created by the different scales. The consideration of these design issues had no structural impact on the engineering of the pyramidal mass, being appended to, but not consolidated within it. The manner in which stairs and ramps were integrated with the mass would arise from the perceived function of the pyramid and from aesthetic percepts, but not from structural necessity.

Stairs and ramps are functional in that they are constructed for human use, however few the original participants may have been, and must be designed to human scale. An interesting anomaly in the notion that stairs indicate human participation can be found in those ancient Maya "pyramids" constructed in the so-called Río Bec style. They are found in the Mexican state of Campeche, in the middle of the Yucatán peninsula. Here, the principal building is a range-type structure. This is a walled structure containing adjoining rooms with significant amounts of interior space, and is often considered to be a palace. At the sites of Río Bec and nearby Xpuhil, range-type structures are each embellished with a group of three pyramids that rise in a symmetrical pattern out of the plan of the palace. Each pyramid has "stairs" that are impossibly steep and that rise to a solidly massed "temple" bearing a dramatic but useless door. One hesitates to characterize these structures as false pyramids, but certainly they were not designed for human use. It is clear that they were built as almost full-scale reproductions of pyramids, but their inaccessibility and their direct association with range-type structures makes it difficult to understand what the original builders had hoped to achieve. Analogies come to mind, such as stage sets, or the careful re-creation of ruins popular in 18th-century European garden design, or copies of architectural forms made, however, for very different purposes. In today's terms one thinks, for example, of the many grand government buildings and museums lining the Mall in Washington, D.C., that are fashioned after Classical Greek temples or Imperial Roman baths.

The Río Bec "pyramids" represent a reuse of form in a self-consciously altered manner, the reasons for which cannot now be determined. Better than any evidence to the contrary, they are the exceptions that prove the rule. They look like pyramids, they are the same size as pyramids, but they are always described as "false," or models, or as substitutions, and the only difference between them and "real" pyramids is that they are designed to be inaccessible.

As with stairs appended to the pyramid, the same functional and aesthetic concerns would be brought to bear on other kinds of exterior embellishments,

Pyramids with no apparent role or function have been found in Mesoamerica. At the Yucatán site of Xpuhil, three solid masonry towers, or "pyramids," adorn the building known as Structure 1. In this reconstruction, by the renowned scholar Tatiana Proskouriakoff, impossibly steep stairways lead up each of the pyramids to a purely ornamental temple on the top.

such as balustrades, cornices, moldings, and doorways to temples (if part of the pyramid profile). This brings the discussion into issues of cultural styles, whereby pyramids are recognized as Cambodian or Mexican or Mayan or Egyptian. The Egyptian pyramid has no external stair or embellishments of any kind: its mass is composed into a monumental geometric form that fully realized for the ancient Egyptian its structural necessities, its perceived function, and its aesthetic requirements. The Egyptian pyramid form may appeal to modern Western aesthetics because through it form and function are just about as integrated as they are ever going to get.

Little remains of the exterior compositions of Sumerian ziggurats and the Ziggurat of Ur, as reconstructed by Sir Leonard Woolley between 1929 and 1939, is our best guide. Constructed with adobe bricks, it was faced with the

Sir Leonard Woolley began the reconstruction of the Ziggurat of Ur in 1929, having first studied and recorded all its existing remains. Shown below is the first and largest of the reconstruction's three stages. The battered exterior profile is broken by regularly placed projecting vertical panels. In each panel of the lower stage, Woolley found (and reconstructed) openings that he termed "weeper-holes". These were thought to have been connected to a "hanging garden" similar to the one that was thought to have later existed at Babylon (*right*). This theory has been discounted, and today the function of the holes remains a mystery.

more durable baked bricks set with bitumen, an oily, tar-like substance. The first and largest stage rose with a battered profile, its exterior surfaces broken by projecting vertical panels repeated at regular intervals. These are usually called buttresses because they are similar to the way city or temple walls were designed. In plan, such walls look like cogs with alternating notches and niches, and their buttressing was functional. On the ziggurat, the vertical panels look more conventional than functional. Woolley also found what he called "weeper-holes" which penetrated the brick facing and were situated with regular frequency in the first stage. The holes look functional rather than decorative, and for that reason Woolley suggested that the first-stage terrace was planted with a "hanging garden". The need to water the garden would explain the presence of weeper-holes. Today, the existence of the hypothetical garden is generally discounted, and the function of the weeper-holes remains a mystery.

The contrasting contours of the three stairways on the first stage of the Ziggurat of Ur, shown here in its reconstructed state, offer an interesting break in the repetitious design of the buttresses. The stairways led first to a covered gateway at the entrance to the second stage, or terrace, and eventually to the temple that dramatically crowned the structure.

The most important exterior design of the ziggurat's first stage is the triple stairway, described in Chapter 2. It marks and focuses attention toward the northeast face, and by its contrasting angle of rise, breaks and relieves the monumental repetition of the buttresses on the battered angle of the mass. The stairs direct the eye toward, and give physical access to, the climactic meeting of the three stairs and the potent rise beyond to the temple of the utmost stage.

The complexity of the Indian exteriors is in direct contrast with the simplicity of the Egyptian and Sumerian exteriors. How the mass of the stupas at Sanchi were originally finished is unknown, but for all stupas, the gates, the railings, and the walls of the processionals would be carved with representational narratives from the life of Buddha. Borobodur may be an extreme example of the stupa, and the same extreme quality of surface richness overwhelms the visitor to Angkor Wat in Cambodia.

Both of these structures are built from symmetrical plans that resemble mandalas, and in plan, both participate in the inherent logic of symmetry. They rise from their mandalas in successive stages, but each stage is designed to appear as if it, too, were constructed by horizontal layers: stacks of cornices and stringcourses of varying projection and design. Intricate organic designs and animal forms (often serpents, or *nagas*) embellish the

architectural frames—balustrades, tympana, lintels, and jambs—that mark stairs, gates, and niches. Within the processional galleries of both Angkor Wat and Borobodur, panels of relief-carved narratives instruct the pilgrim as he or she proceeds through the monument.

There is a creative tension between the logic of the plan and the experience of participating in the architectural elevations. The experience is one of extremes, from darkened gallery to brightness of sun; from the clear vistas of the towers to their eclipse behind stages as one moves closer to the center; from low to high, from stair, to gate, to terrace, to gallery. The close, experiential effect is labyrinthine. The pilgrim must have faith that out of confusion clarity will arise. The more distant and studied effect of the plan is its rational symmetry. Art historian Nelson Wu speaks of this most poignantly when he describes the pilgrim's approach to, and interaction with, a stupa. From a distance, the pilgrim sees the silhouette of the whole structure, "its strong general statements.... It is the primary revelation of

Although no historical relationship exists between the pyramids of Mesoamerica and those of Southeast Asia, the thick forests of Cambodia and Guatemala both enclose temple-towers with many common features. Temple I at Tikal (*left*), reveals many structural features that seemingly parallel those of the temples of Angkor Wat (*above*). The elaborate roof adornment known as a roof comb, common to Mayan structures, bears strong resemblance to the ornately decorated roofing of the Cambodian temple-towers.

truth to be followed by agonizing paths in which one loses sight of it until the time of final salvation."

In ancient Mesoamerica, pyramid plans, whether they were circular, square, or rectangular, show no obvious formal relationship to the mandala-plans of India and Southeast Asia. However, in the stepped elevation and in exterior embellishments, comparisons can be, and have been, drawn. It should be pointed out that such comparisons are made by Westerners following their own aesthetic responses that prompt them to see similarities, especially between the temple-towers in the rain forests of Cambodia and the ancient pyramids in the Guatemalan jungles. Both of these traditions dictated complex exterior embellishments made up of organic and animal forms, and both also represented narratives in low relief in gallery passages associated with the pyramid. Both Asian and Mesoamerican builders used the corbeled arch but this fact would have greater comparative impact were it not that all pyramid-builders used the corbel where small interior spaces are involved.

Maya and Mexican pyramids were usually topped by temples, few of which have survived. However, a fully restored temple can be seen atop the pyramid at Santa Cecilia Acatitlán, a suburb of Mexico City. The one-room temple has a single doorway and a decorated, trapezoidal roof, and is considered typical of Aztec construction. It is set back on the pyramid's upper platform, leaving room for religious rituals in front.

The exterior embellishments of the Mesoamerican stepped and staired pyramid can be grouped into two major styles: Maya and Mexican. The Maya pyramid rises by staged and battered steps that are embellished by thin moldings and aprons of differing proportions, with the occasional addition of repeating outset panels. The balustrades framing the stairs are often decorated with a repeating design evocative of the serpent. In comparison to Khmer architecture, this part of the Maya pyramid is restrained. The ancient Maya would decorate the temple atop the pyramid with fantastic designs, most often in painted stucco, covering the wide entablatures and doorways of the upper zones. As a finishing touch they would adorn the roof with a flying panel, called a roof comb, rising vertically into the sky. The roof comb could support any number of complex stucco designs interweaving organic, animal, and human images. The use of stucco to smooth the surfaces of both the staged platform and the complexities of the temple imagery imparts a plastic and unified sculptural quality to the Maya pyramid no matter what its scale.

The Mexican pyramid is more restrained than the Maya and is seldom used as a comparison to Khmer architecture. The art historian Donald Robertson points out that rather than being unified like the Maya pyramid, the Mexican pyramid was conceived as a series of repeating units. He calls it "unitary composition": the talud-tablero of Teotihuacán's pyramids is a good example.

Few temples built atop the Mexican pyramid have survived. They are known to have existed because postholes are evident on some summits. Our best information comes from descriptions of late Mexica or Aztec culture

Although the trend would change by about the second century A.D., early Maya pyramids were decorated with painted stucco masks and emblems that surrounded the stepped stages and framed the stairs. The pyramid at Cerros, in Belize, is a fine example of this style. Later exteriors, however, were more austere, with ornament applied only to the temple atop the pyramid.

sketched and written in chronicles dating from shortly after the Conquest, and because the recently excavated Templo Mayor of Tenochtitlán (now Mexico City) preserved in its heartings the twin-temple walls belonging to the second rebuilding (circa A.D. 1400). At Tenayuca and Tenochtitlán, pyramids supported twin temples approached by a double stairway on the west face. (It is not generally supposed that the tradition of double temples extends much earlier into Mexican prehistory.) Each temple was a one-room structure topped by an extended entablature rising like a roof comb. Illustrations in the chronicles show the entablatures framing repeated abstract designs, probably worked in stucco, of small nodules or hemispheres interspersed with human skulls and small inset squares or niches. Robertson's term, unitary, seems to be a proper one for the exterior designs, in that they consist of one or two abstract forms repeated in a symmetrical design.

Although the typical Mexican pyramid looks as if it were made from building blocks varying in proportion, but not in form, there are enough exceptions to this general description to make one wonder about the many 20th-century restorations and reconstructions that have been realized. At the turn of the century, the great Pyramid of the Sun was "excavated" with dynamite and all traces of its outer facings have been lost. The main ceremonial complex of the later Toltec capital city of Tula, northwest of Teotihuacán, was restored during the 1930s, a restoration influenced by the current theories about its close connections with the Maya site of Chichén Itzá. Few scholars today would question these connections, but they have since developed different ideas about how the connections actually worked, which raise questions about some aspects of the restorations. However,

Chichén Itzá also was undergoing excavation and restoration at the same time as Tula. At both sites, the restorative solutions, especially for the Temple of the Warriors at Chichén Itzá and Pyramid B at Tula, took on circular, tautological qualities wherein the expectations that similar forms existed at both sites may have produced similar forms in reconstructions, particularly when the archaeological record was thin.

There are indications that the willingness to decorate the exteriors of pyramids was an early aesthetic in Mesoamerica, and one that gave way to an increasing simplicity or, really, a greater explicitness of forms. The Temple of Quetzalcóatl, or the Feathered Serpent, at Teotihuacán, the third great pyramid to be built at the site, was initially designed (circa A.D. 150) with exuberant exterior sculptures of mythical animal heads projecting out from its tableros and joined by a low relief of an undulating serpent body—all brilliantly painted in a wide range of colors. Between A.D. 350 and 450, this highly expressive facade was covered over with an extension, called an *adosada*, composed with plain units of taluds and tableros. Most of the public buildings that can be seen at Teotihuacán today have this same austere, unitary exterior, originally painted a monochrome red or white, and they follow the change in aesthetics that can be seen in the remodeling of the Temple of the Feathered Serpent.

Similarly, the earliest Maya pyramids were decorated with brilliantly painted stucco masks and emblems ranging around the stepped stages and framing the stairs. The pyramids at Cerros, Lamanai, and Uaxactún are beautiful examples of this early decorative method. This gradually gave way to more austere exteriors wherein the stucco sculpture-work was reserved for the temples high atop the pyramids.

ECONOMICS OF MONUMENTALITY

Without the interior reinforcements of iron and steel that are employed in modern architecture, there are structural limits to the heights that can be achieved by piling up dirt or laying courses of adobe and stone. Nonetheless, even with the materials available to them, ancient pyramid-builders somehow always exceeded modern expectations about ancient capabilities. Modern interests in, and puzzlements over, the ancient monumental achievements center on the necessary economics and energies required to achieve such forms. These include the building materials and technical resources available to the builders, as well as the economics and energies related to human resources, which we must still consider.

When asked how long it took to build a pyramid, the usual answer given by archaeologists is 50 years. This is the estimate that has been given separately for the Great Pyramid of Khufu (Cheops), for the massive Pyramid of the Sun at Teotihuacán, and the monumental temple complex of Angkor Wat—all three built in very different times, with very different materials and construction techniques. Nonetheless, all three pyramids rose through the expenditure of human energy alone; that is, the monuments were the work of preindustrial peoples, who may have had draft animals for assistance (except in Mesoamerica), and whose only mechanical aids were levers and, possibly, the use of pulleys. Given this fact, it seems logical that, regardless of the date or the materials and techniques used, it would take about the same amount of time—one and one-half generations—to build a "mountain" using only human energy and resources.

What are the human resources necessary? In other words, what does it take to build a mountain? First of all, we suppose that the marshaling of a labor force large enough to successfully complete a monumental project such as a pyramid would require a "surplus economy". That is, the workers had to be fed, if not paid, for their labor. Their energies, directed toward construction not sustenance, would require that food be supplied by others who could produce enough food for themselves, as well as for others. This presumes that the technologies of agriculture were sufficient to produce a surplus, and that there was a social agreement of some kind as to who should manage the surplus, and how. The terms of this agreement can range from being the imposition of the will and dictates of a state to the communal decisions made at a local level. One suspects that such agreements were actually a combination wherein the impositions of the larger governmental institutions (whether organized as states, confederations, or chiefdoms) on the smaller, local groups would have to be sensitive and, in some way accommodate, the local decisions about surplus. Furthermore, accommodation between potentially conflicting ideas about how to manage an agricultural surplus would be essential for the success of monumental projects requiring the energies of so large a body of the citizenry for such long periods as can be counted in generations.

Hollywood-type visions of an army of starving slaves groaning under cracking whips to satisfy the megalomania of a pharaoh are merely celluloid fictions. For many years, archaeologists and historians have demonstrated how cooperation and accommodation, rather than imposition and coercion, were the necessary means for feeding and organizing the labor force that was required for the construction of great architectural projects. Ancient inscriptions, left as identification marks by the quarriers and stonemasons themselves, record that the "Vigorous Gang" and the "Enduring Gang" worked at the Egyptian pyramids, and their chosen names suggest a quality of solidarity and pride. The excavation of Egyptian workers' villages demonstrates that they lived with their families and offers clues as to what they ate, where they celebrated and worshipped, and also where they were buried. Studies of bones (osteology) show that the food they ate and the lives they led—they often died young—were less than ideal, but the villages they inhabited were not slave quarters. Recently, Zahi Hawass, General

The tremendous amounts of resources and manpower required for the construction of Egypt's massive monuments has been a source of fascination ever since the initial discovery of these structures. In a painting entitled *Israel in Egypt*, the 19th-century British painter Sir Edward Poynter shows gangs of Israelites hauling enormous statues into position under the lash of their Egyptian masters. This old-fashioned portrayal of the way the pyramids and other monuments were built is probably not accurate, but has shaped our view of Egyptian civilization.

Antiquities Director for the Great Pyramids and Sphinx of Giza, has been excavating the quarters of the laborers who built the Great Pyramids.

Besides being fed, housed, and/or paid, a large labor force requires a great deal of organization. This requires work gangs responsible for certain jobs, and this in turn requires management and overseers who know how to look after and handle the work force, as well as being responsible for the distribution the jobs at the right time and place. Overseers would work with (and probably ultimately answer to) the professionals—the astronomers, architects, engineers, masons, and priests. In ancient Egypt, it is thought that many laborers and their overseers were seasonal workers, joining the work force during the summer months while the Nile was flooding. No agricultural work could be done, and farmers could join the monumental project as unskilled or semiskilled labor.

Very little information about the labor force and managerial organization involved in other pyramid projects is available. In 16th-century Peru, however, Pedro de Cieza de León wrote of how the Temple-Fortress of

Sacsahuamán was built by a labor force that, in addition to four architects, comprised 20,000 men, including quarrymen, transport workers, masons, carpenters, and professional foremen.

Twenty thousand semiskilled and skilled laborers seems like a reasonable estimate for the Sacsahuamán labor force. Herodotus gives a figure of 100,000 for the number of workers on the Egyptian pyramids. Kurt Mendelssohn considers this figure too high and calculates a permanent, thus professional and skilled, work force of around 10,000 to 20,000 men, increasing to approximately 70,000 during key stages of the building process, and/or when such numbers were available during the agricultural off-season.

What impresses modern students of the various pyramid projects is the organizational abilities of the ancient builders and patrons of the monumental projects. Such phrases as "unsurpassed organizing talent" and "the best organizers of human labor the world has ever seen" are used to describe the ancient Egyptians. Indeed, Kurt Mendelssohn considers that the greatest talent displayed by Imhotep as he built the first stepped pyramid (Zoser's Complex at Saqqara) was his organizational skill, not his innovative design.

It is logical to think that all pyramid construction required such essential organizational talents. But in fact more was needed. Having the wherewithal, the organizational abilities to marshal the material and economic resources, and the requisite labor force, does not in itself mean a pyramid will be built. There must also be the desire to build a pyramid, together with an idea of how its ideological purposes are to be embedded in the construction and design. And this is where the architect enters the picture. Most commonly, the patron of an ancient monument is spoken of as if he or she were the architect or the builder: "Pacal built his temple in the center of Palenque," for example. Pacal was the ruler of Palenque at the time the Temple of Inscriptions was built there in the seventh century, and the inscriptions found within the pyramid all point to the fact that he was the patron, the person who desired to have it built. Surely, he had a lot to say about what ideologies and functions it was to serve, but it seems unlikely that he worked out the designs. He must have employed an architect.

To speak of the patron as the builder is to relegate the practice of building to craft; that is, there were no professional resources, only traditional ones to draw upon. Although history has left us very few architects' names, the pyramids themselves tell us that the complexities involved in matching ideology with construction, and the astoundingly beautiful solutions achieved, must have come from the genius of architects dedicated to the profession of building. The economics of genius is not a common subject, and little more can be said about the architects who labored at building pyramids, but no pyramid arose sui generis just because a people had the ability to make one. Each pyramid built represents a unique combination of human capability, intelligence, desire, and decision.

Dedicated to the goddess of heaven, the Eanna Ziggurat at Uruk, in present-day Iraq, was once surrounded by extensive courtyards and terraces. easily eroded, its form is barely recognizable. Nearby are the remains of the Anu Ziggurat, with its White Temple dedicated to Anu, god of

FUNCTIONS AND IDEOLOGIES

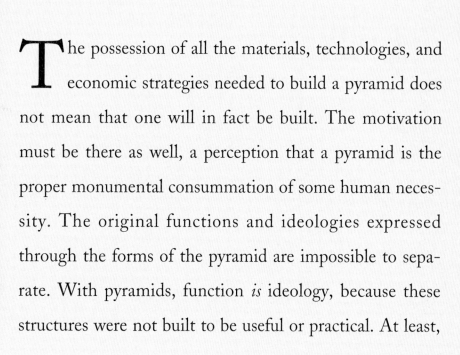

The possession of all the materials, technologies, and economic strategies needed to build a pyramid does not mean that one will in fact be built. The motivation must be there as well, a perception that a pyramid is the proper monumental consummation of some human necessity. The original functions and ideologies expressed through the forms of the pyramid are impossible to separate. With pyramids, function *is* ideology, because these structures were not built to be useful or practical. At least,

Because the ziggurat's sunbaked mud bricks are heaven.

they did not provide shelter from the weather, nor were they used to store food. The ideologies they served, however, can be described as functioning to mark a place and to make manifest an ideal.

MARKING PLACE

By their overriding size and visibility, pyramids mark and solemnize a place in an absolute way—at the time they were built and forever after, as long as they stand. Today, the ancient pyramid often is used as a symbol, a figure of speech for the totality of a particular cultural history. An image of the great Pyramid of Khufu can evoke all of ancient Egyptian history and, likewise, the image of Angkor Wat's temple-towers rising out of the rain forest can stand for the mysteries of the entire Khmer civilization.

An original function within several, but not all, pyramid traditions, however, was to mark the burial of an eminent person: Mesoamerican, Egyptian, and Chinese pyramids are known to have served this purpose. The Khmer temple-towers of Angkor Wat may have been markers for burials, and the Buddhist

An individual of the Khmer civilization who performed great deeds during his lifetime could achieve the status of a god-king, or Cakravartin. Although Khmer temples were seldom actual burial sites, they nevertheless were adorned with reminders of a god-king's greatness. The sculpted image of one such individual appears throughout the Angkor complex, and adorns all four sides of this tower.

The falcon-headed god Horus, son of Osiris, embodied the person of the living pharaoh, as is evident in this wall painting from the great burial complex located in the Valley of Kings, Lower Egypt. In death, the pharaoh became Osiris, the underworld god.

stupa, although not a burial, refers by its form to burial architecture. At this time, only the ziggurats of Sumeria and the great platforms of South America do not show a primary connection with the burial process.

But even with Egyptian pyramids, burial was never the only motivation behind their construction. The fact that a dead person was honored in such a monumental fashion is evidence of personal aggrandizement on a tremendous scale. Such a display would at least require community acceptance of, if not belief in, the propriety and correctness of this show of grandeur. Although there were exceptions, as a rule pyramid burials were reserved for those considered divine—humans who because of their exalted birth or great deeds had achieved the status of a god-king. This is how the texts of ancient Egypt, Khmer Cambodia, and Q'in China are translated to describe the patrons and supposed inhabitants of their pyramids. Some royal burials found within the ancient Maya pyramids are now thought to be those of divine kings, because the recent ability of scholars to read ancient Maya texts appears to substantiate the inference of divinity. But I would like to add a word of caution. As with so many ancient texts, the ancient Maya glyphs are not written in a way that allows us to interpret their meaning precisely. Instead, meaning must be inferred from context. An assumption of divinity may lead to misconstruing certain texts through a priori expectations.

Interestingly enough, it is the Buddhist stupa that most clearly expresses the idea of the god-king, even though it supposedly did not function as an actual burial. Buddha was a human who attained the godlike Cakravartin, or world-ruler, status through his earthly deeds. His relics are traditionally believed to have been "buried" in the stupas, and thus his physical remains and effects were seemingly dispersed like Osiris's broken body. In Egyptian myth, Osiris is the underworld god who was brutally murdered by his brother, Seth, his corpse hacked to pieces and scattered over the landscape. Osiris's wife, Isis, patiently traveled great distances and endured many hardships until she managed to collect her husband's remains and have them buried whole. And finally, Osiris's son, Horus, the falcon-headed god, revenged his father by defeating his uncle. During the Old Kingdom, the living pharaoh was the embodiment of Horus; in death, pharaoh was Osiris. Is there some kind of ideological similarity between the dispersed relics of Buddha and the dead pharaoh as Osiris? There are reasons for speculation. The forms of the early stupas of Sanchi are the only ones that match the inaccessibility of the Egyptian pyramid as a place for human use. That the Egyptian pyramid may have originally been intended, like the stupa, to house the relics of a deity—in this case pharaoh as Osiris—may have a bearing on the fact that Old Kingdom pharaohs had built at least two pyramids each, perhaps to house the dispersed relics of their Osirin identities achieved at death.

The ancient Egyptian kings built two major pyramids and several subsidiary ones generally thought to honor and mark the burial of their consorts. Of the two major structures, it is supposed that one was for actual burial and the other was a cenotaph, or symbolic place of burial. The perceived need was to commemorate the ruler's death in both Upper Egypt (in the south) and Lower Egypt (in the north). Later commentators add that the construction of two tombs was a strategy intended to discourage tomb robbers from desecrating the burial, because they would not know which tomb actually contained the corpse and the goods. However, few corpses, and none that have been identified as rulers, have been found in a pyramid burial. It should be noted, however, that during the later Egyptian times of the Saïte Dynasty (26th Dynasty; 663-525 B.C.), there was a reawakened interest in Old Kingdom forms and ideas. Some Old Kingdom pyramids were "restored" and, indeed, reused. The few bodies

On the upper terraces of Borobodur sit 72 miniature stupas, each containing a seated statue of Buddha. Stone lattice-work domes cover the figures, with the openings in the stonework allowing the Buddha inside to be seen and touched. The Buddha shown here is one of two that have lost their latticework covering. The central stupa, which is closed to view, contains a statue of the Supreme Buddha, and may represent the symbolic "burial" of a god-king.

actually found in pyramids built during the Old Kingdom inevitably turn out to have been burials dating from Saïte times.

Sarcophagi, however, have been found in the burial chambers of the pyramids. The most intriguing, and for many the most disappointing, was that found at Saqqara deep within the Unfinished Pyramid of Sekhemket of the Third Dynasty, the ruler who was probably Zoser's successor. The renowned Egyptian archaeologist, Zakaria Goneim, excavated this stepped pyramid in the 1950s. When the burial chamber below the mass of the unfinished pyramid was disclosed with its unopened sarcophagus, great hopes were raised that finally a royal pyramid burial had come to light. The rectangular sarcophagus was carved from one block of alabaster and, instead of having a lid, it was opened by a sliding end panel, still anciently sealed and cemented. When opened, it contained nothing, which is the general

The temples associated with Egyptian pyramids were the focus of the cult of the pharaoh. The Pyramid of Khufu, shown here, was the climax of a processional route that commenced at a Valley Temple close to the floodwaters of the Nile and proceeded via a covered causeway to a Mortuary Temple located at the foot of the pyramid. Here, priests performed the rituals of the ruler's cult.

description of all sarcophagi. They are the place of burial, but no body was held within them—the empty tomb of the deathless divinity.

Without bodies, we cannot be certain that the Old Kingdom Egyptian pyramids functioned primarily as markers for the actual burials of the deceased rulers, but we can be certain they functioned as symbolic markers for ceremonial royal burials. Contemporary hieroglyphic texts and the writings of later but still ancient, commentators such as the Greek historian Herodotus, make this function very clear. It seems proper, then, to consider that the ancient Egyptian pyramids were built primarily as functional expressions of memorial and commemoration. The pyramid manifests a declaration of a communal bond, a kind of contract between the person to be memorialized and the people who would do the remembering. The flourishing of the pharaoh's cult, wherein after the "burial," offerings were continually brought to the overseer-priests who maintained the temples and the rituals associated with the pyramid, seems to be another expression of this contract. Whatever other functions the cenotaph-pyramid fulfills—as a commemorative memorial built and supported by a community—it is a place where ideas, things, and people come together for the purposes of identity and unification.

Pyramids had another important function—the elevation and support of temples—thus making them a focus for ceremony and worship. Temples are regularly found on stepped or staged elevations augmented by stairs or ramps connecting the base of the pyramid to the temple enclosure at its top. In Mesoamerica, pyramids may both support a temple and contain a major burial as well. With what little evidence we have so far, this probably was true also of the temple-towers of the Khmers. In Peru, the grand platforms supported architecture of some kind, but like the temples atop the ziggurats of Sumeria, little remains to tell us what the real function of these architectural forms may have been. Generally, they are thought to have been used for religious purposes.

We have little knowledge of the Sumerian temples built atop ziggurats, except that they are supposed to have been similar in kind to the White Temple found on its high platform atop the so-called Anu Ziggurat, at Uruk in present-day Iraq. Built with thick adobe walls shaped with cog-shaped buttresses inside and out, the interior of the temple consisted of one long, rectangular room flanked by rows of small subsidiary rooms. The temple was entered through a door in the long southwest wall, requiring the pilgrim or priest to turn left toward the altar after entering. This is called the bent-axis approach. The temple was considered the god's house, or as André Parrot poignantly describes it, the "gate of god," or the "gate of heaven." It was where humankind, represented by ruler and priest, and god came together atop the mountain that transcended the earthly realms.

The temples atop the Mesoamerican pyramid are of various plans and designs (as were, most likely, the ziggurat temples). The ones that remain testify that they were never intended as places where people would congregate. They are much smaller spaces than the ziggurat temples. Considering the smallness of these interior spaces, some scholars suggest they were designed only for functional uses, such as storage places for ceremonial paraphernalia; others consider more esoteric purposes, such as private places for initiation rituals or individual penance.

The few ancient Maya temples that have survived allow us to suppose that many temple interiors, while small, were nonetheless beautifully and richly decorated. The temples atop the tall pyramids of Tikal, in the rain forest of Guatemala, were adorned with exquisitely carved lintels over their doors. Zapote, a hard wood resistant to rot and insects, was shaped into panels fitted together and carved with a low and intricate relief depicting humans in mythical contexts. These are understood as "portraits" of the pyramid's ruler-patron, whose likeness is surrounded by gigantic serpents and jaguars that testify to, and defend, his divinity. At approximately the same time, designs carved in limestone and molded in stucco were being placed in the temple above Pacal's tomb at Palenque. After ascending the grand stairs, one enters the Temple of Inscriptions through any one of five doorways separated by piers. The piers are sculptured in stucco, and each displays an adult, male or female, holding a baby—a baby whose left leg is rendered as an undulating serpent. These are understood as depicting ancestors holding Pacal's heir, Chan Bahlum, who is thus clearly divine from birth. Within the temple are three limestone wall panels carved with hieroglyphs, not fully translated, but thought to relate the dynastic history of the realm and of Pacal's life, ending with the accession to rulership of his son, Chan Bahlum.

Present scholarly interpretation focuses on the political implications of dynastic succession and power expressed in these temple texts and images. It is equally true, however, that a "mountain" was raised in stages using the religiously conceived numbers and proportions of four, nine, and thirteen—a fact that strongly suggests ideological percepts. Both pyramids were also markers for materially rich burials that still held the remains of the deceased—no missing bodies here—placed within the heart of the pyramid. The functions expressed by Temple I of Tikal and the Temple of Inscriptions at Palenque, encapsulate both political and transcendental or transformational metaphors.

Because of its placement over a natural cave, the Pyramid of the Sun at Teotihuacán clearly marked a place anciently perceived as having geomantic and earthly potency. The closest analogies for this kind of marking are Greek temples and ancient Peruvian huacas. In his book, *The Earth, the Temple, and the Gods*, Vincent Scully convincingly depicts the Greek temple as commemorating and marking the natural features of springs, tree groves, and mountains. The huaca, as a place of power, was sometimes left in its natural state and sometimes marked by carvings on natural rocks or by some kind of structure. Neither the temple nor the huaca qualifies as a pyramid, and it may be that the geomantic marking function expressed by the Pyramid of the Sun was more usually declared by other kinds of monuments. Plans of pyramids oriented according to celestial movements, especially those of the sun, are conceptually related to the marking of a place known for its geomantic potency. As concrete manifestations of natural powers and cycles, both these kinds of marking acknowledge or allow for communication and connection between the natural and human worlds.

An important function for the pyramid, then, was to mark and commemorate a place. The place could be the burial, actual or symbolic, of a divine person or a place for worship signaled by the temple raised to the heavens, or both. By marking places believed to hold earthly powers or, more commonly, by aligning the pyramid's plans to celestial cycles, the pyramid aligns with, and thus reveals, the orders of the natural world and the universe. In its

All pyramids were sited to take account of celestial events—whether equinoctial, solstitial, or stellar. An alignment of Jupiter and Venus over Temple I at Tikal, Guatemala, provides evidence that some Maya pyramids were oriented to the passage of Venus.

functions as burial marker and temple support, the pyramid explicitly was a place of communal energies, identity, and unity. Implicitly, it was a place where connections were made between the earth and the cosmos, life and death, human and god, between experience and hope.

THE IDEAL MADE MANIFEST

A pyramid functioned as a concrete or manifest expression of ideology. But the ideologies thus expressed are seldom explicit, and because we cannot precisely define them, we must infer their meaning. While the pyramid's function as a marker can be generalized as "drawing human connections," its function as manifesting an ideal can be generalized as an "affirmation of order." In his book, *The Art and Architecture of India*, the art historian Benjamin Rowland discusses the ancient Indian concept of *pratibimba* that encompasses this function of expressed ideology. Pratibimba is the making of an "immanent symbol," and "the reconstruction in architecture or sculpture of the imagined structure of supernatural things or regions...." With the form of the pyramid, this manifestation of the symbolic was actually achieved on three levels: structurally, where the pyramid was designed as a microcosm of the greater universe; concretely, because it provided instruction for the attainment of perfect order; and aesthetically, as the formal embodiment of perfection.

The macrocosmic cycles of the sun and stars were important to the proper sighting of all pyramids: all plans reflect in their orientations either the cardinal directions dominated by equinoctial east-west directions, solstitial solar events, or, finally, by stellar events. Most commonly, the pyramid and its temple, if there was one, would be oriented with the cardinal directions, revealing either the cardinal points or the intercardinal points. If the plan were square, it would reflect both: when the sides are cardinal, the points are intercardinal and vice versa.

Cardinal directions are given symbolic meanings by all peoples, and while these vary from culture to culture, the most important, and most easily calculated, directions are east and west, where the sun rises and sets. East and west are the places of birth and death. Different cultures will amplify these meanings in different ways, but it is almost universal for peoples to equate birth with the rising of the sun in the east and its setting in the west with death. North and south are more difficult directions to calculate and have much wider variations of meanings. In Mesoamerica, scholars are beginning to think that north and south were not the cardinal, or important, directions for the ancient peoples, but rather the sun's reaching zenith in the center of the sky and, conversely, the unseen nadir beneath the earth. The scholar Anagarika Govinda's description of the formal symbolism of the Buddhist stupa implies a similar construction of the cardinal directions: east-west and up-down rather than north-south. However, the Egyptian interest in the north node is clearly reflected in the direction and angle of the interior passageways to (or from) the tombs beneath the pyramids. For the ancient Egyptian, north symbolized the place of eternal life where the stars never rise or set but endlessly circle around the north node of the sky.

The sides of the Egyptian pyramids are almost perfectly oriented to the cardinal directions. This is in contrast to the sides of the Sumerian ziggurat which are oriented along the intercardinal points. Both traditions reveal the intention to orient the pyramid cardinally: the Egyptians evoke the cardinals in a static, positive relationship, while the Sumerians evoke a diagonal and more dynamic one. Why they differed in this could either be circumstantial or more deeply rooted in cultural aesthetics. One can argue that the ziggurat was a place of human activity and ceremony in contrast to the enclosed final form of the Egyptian pyramid, which, as it were, repelled the presence of humans. This may or may not have had something to do with the microcosmic reflection of a static or dynamic universe.

Solstitial events—the rising and setting of the sun in its most northerly and southerly positions as seen on the horizon—were another inspiration for orientation of plan. This is best known in ancient Mesoamerica where recent scholarship has provided measured observations for several pyramids. Actually, Mesoamerican pyramids can coalesce in their elevations and temples equinoctial and solstitial, as well as stellar, events.

At Uaxactún, in the heart of the Guatemalan rain forest near Tikal, a beautiful stucco-covered pyramid was constructed sometime during the first century B.C. Rising in five uneven stages from a square plan, the balustrades framing its four stairs centered on its four sides were sculptured with great deity heads. The stairs and sides of the pyramid reflect equally the cardinal points. The temple on the top, however, faced east across a plaza bounded by low platforms thus giving preference to this direction. Over time, the pyramid and the platforms were reconstructed and the stuccoed sculptures on the pyramid were covered over. Nonetheless, the cardinal orientation was faithfully maintained. During the third century A.D. three small temples were erected on the eastern platform that faced the pyramid across the plaza. By standing in the middle of the pyramid's eastern stairs, an observer could watch the equinoctial sun rise over the small central temple, the summer solstice sunrise marked by the far edge of the southern temple, and the winter solstice marked by the far edge of the little northern temple. The pyramid itself reifies the cardinal directions and "points to" both equinoctial and solstitial events. The Mesoamerican propensity to express geometry and design by line of sight is clearly at work here.

At Teotihuacán in the central Valley of Mexico, the Pyramid of the Sun faces west, not east. The orientation of its western face, as mentioned in Chapter 2, is an odd 15 degrees north of west, but this allows someone standing on its grand central stairway to watch the zenith sun set directly in front them. Importantly, the setting of the zenith sun was directly presaged by the star cluster of the

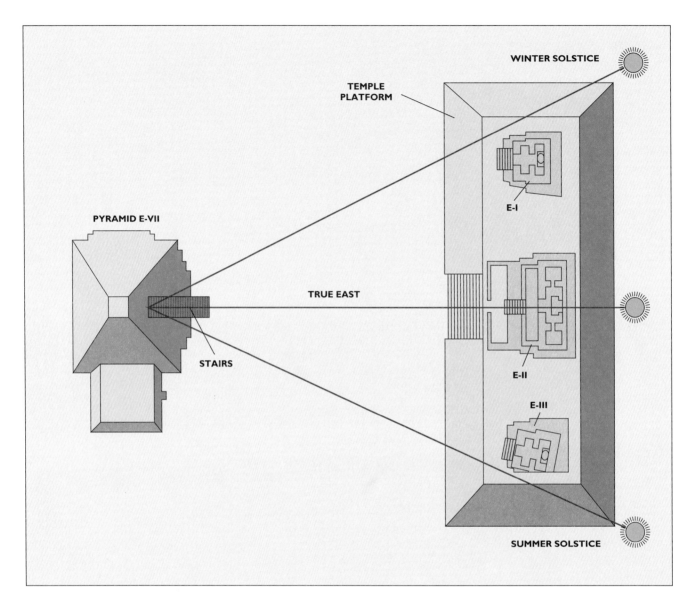

The importance of solar events to the Maya is evident in the orientation of the pyramid complex at Uaxactún, Guatemala. An observer on Pyramid E-VII looking east toward three small temples would see the equinoctial sun rise over the central temple, while the summer and winter solstice sunrises would appear at the edge of the southern and northern temples respectively.

Pleiades on the day of their heliacal rising and setting. (Heliacal refers to the position and time when stars and planets rise or set closest to the sun but are still visible.) The western front and stairs of the later Mexican pyramid at Tenayuca are also thought to be oriented to the heliacal passage of the Pleiades, and offer one more example of the ancient American interest in this star group.

A difference in orientation can be detected between the ancient Maya pyramid, which manifests (and marks, as well) either equinoctial or solstitial (cardinal) events often keyed to the passages of the planet Venus, and the ancient Mexican pyramid, which manifests the passage of the zenith (and

The annual flooding of the Nile nourished the civilization of ancient Egypt, one of whose legends held that a water lily growing on a mound of earth exposed by the receding floodwaters was the source of the sun. At Heliopolis, center of the Egyptian cult of the sun, a cone-shaped stone was enshrined as a reminder of the mound. Some scholars have suggested that this was the proto-type of the Egyptian pyramid.

nadir) sun keyed to the movements of the Pleiades. This, of course, is a broad generalization that will not hold for all Mexican and Maya pyramids.

Another structural connection between the macrocosmic universe and the microcosm of human endeavor is revealed by the pervasive symbolism that equates the pyramid to a mountain. Like the symbolic meanings attributed to the cardinal directions, the pyramid-mountain is variously described in ancient cultures, but in general it was understood in two ways: as the world-mountain at the center and beginning of the world and/or as the holy mountain where the gods dwell. The function of the ideology behind the pyramid-as-mountain is to connect the actualities of human experience to human understandings about the universe that are beyond possible experience. The artificial mountain built by humankind has its base in the existential world, its roots in the under-world, and rises to the heavens. It should be mentioned that many pyramids are described in myths and folk stories as having a mirror image of its mass constructed underground below its base.

The Egyptian "mountain" refers to the first creation-event, when a mound rose out of the chaos of primeval waters. I.E.S. Edwards states in his seminal book, *The Pyramids of Egypt*, that the appearance of this mythical first mound is re-enacted each year when the floodwaters of the Nile begin to recede and the first muddy bumps of land appear. During the first creation-event, a water lily grew on this mound, and from it came the sun with its powers of generation and life.

The White Temple at Uruk, in present-day Iraq, sits atop the high platform known as the Anu Ziggurat. This cutaway illustration shows the temple constructed with one long pillared room flanked by small subsidiary chambers. For the ancient Sumerians, the temple was a house at the summit of a mountain, where ruler and priest, representing the people, met with their god.

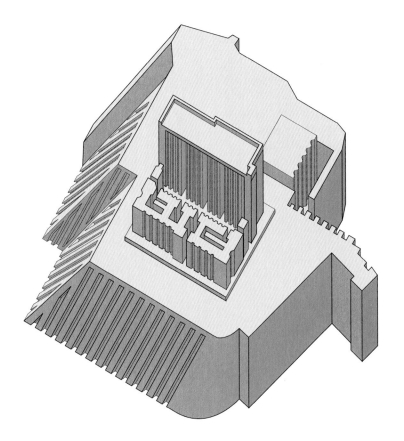

Heliopolis was the center of the sun religion during the Old Kingdom, and inside the temple dedicated to the sun, a sacred object was kept—a conically shaped stone known as the *ben-ben*. Supposedly symbolizing the mound of the first creation-event, the ben-ben has been cited by many students as a prototype for the pyramid. The relationship between the ben-ben and the pyramid is formal, but as archaeologist Ahmed Fakhry points out, it is hard to understand what the relationship may have been between the ben-ben and sun worship. In this case, Fakhry recites the poetic explanation that the ben-ben and the pyramid each represent "the appearance of the sun's rays shining through a break in the clouds, which look like gigantic pyramids connecting heaven with earth." This empirical and impressionistic explanation probably was initiated by J.H. Breasted in 1912, and was echoed later in the work of I.E.S. Edwards.

The Egyptian pyramid-as-mountain is also referred to as a ramp or, in the case of stepped pyramids, a stairway to be used by the deceased to ascend to the heavenly realm of the gods. This is a metaphoric function, of course, and could not be extended to anyone living, given the hugeness of the steps or the steepness of the ramps.

The Sumerians designed their pyramid-mountains to enable human participation. Ziggurats were understood as artificial mountains that aspired to the heavens, sometimes characterized as "ladders" leading to the "gate of heaven" manifested as the temple. Significantly, however, ziggurats were also conceived as places with the right kind of attraction that might compel deities to descend to earth. In fact, André Parrot considers that out of the Sumerian and Babylonian desires for their god to appear, witnessed through their prayers for calling the deity to come before them, the Christian concept of god incarnate arose. From contemporary texts, however, the ziggurat-mountain is discussed as a place of transaction, a "marriage" between humankind and deity, and its formal designs positively reflect this function.

While the ziggurat-mountain reaches to the heavens to allow the ascent of humankind or the descent of the gods, the mythical Mount Meru, embodied within the form of the stupa, was more like Mount Olympus of the ancient Greeks in being the residence for certain eternal deities. The mass of the early stupa, however, does not have stairs or temples, and the only place for human transaction is in the processional path between the railing and the base. Although many commentators believe the world-axis, or *axis mundi*, is synonymous with the world-mountain and embedded in its symbolism, the stupa's mast (*yasti*) makes this connection

The earliest stupas were surrounded by a wooden fence, or *vedika*, with entrances at the cardinal points. In later stupas, stone vedikas replaced wooden ones, but the undecorated stone vedika that surrounds the Great Stupa at Sanchi, India (*right*), was clearly meant to suggest a wooden construction. The function of the vedika was to separate the sacred precinct from the secular world. Rising high above the dome of Swayambu Stupa, in Kathmandu, Nepal (*above*), the *yasti* (mast) symbolizes the world axis rising from the primordial waters. The tiers of the mast represent the *devalokas*, or heavens of the gods, culminating in the heaven of Brahma.

The *huaca* (sacred place) of Kenko, a carved limestone outcrop in the valley basin of Cuzco, Peru, was one of 328 shrines positioned on the 41 *ceques*, or conceptual radial lines, traced from the center of the Inca capital of Cuzco. The ceques were the expression of Incaic ideas about religion, social organization, calendrics, and astronomy. Huacas were sited in fields, on riverbanks, over springs or natural wells, as well as on carved rock formations such as Kenko.

explicit. The temple-towers of the Khmer are also world-mountains, representing the Indian Mount Meru and the axis mundi.

The contemporary texts, as well as mythical stories recorded by later ethnographers in Mesoamerica, are not as explicit in calling the pyramid a mountain. The inference, however, seems unavoidable. The first major pyramid to be built in Mesoamerica, at La Venta, was shaped like a volcano. The later, staged pyramids usually rise by four or nine steps, sometimes five

and thirteen—all significant numerals in ancient descriptions of the universe. The four "cardinal" directions represented by four stages would put the temple at the fifth stage, referring to the center of the world where the directionals cross. There are nine descriptive levels in the underworld, presided over by the "nine lords of the night." Five stages were probably used when no temple was constructed on the top of the pyramid, and so refers to the same central, axial place taken by the temple atop four stages. (The so-called "twin-pyramids" at Tikal are raised five stages with no evidence of temples. They probably functioned as platforms for ceremonial dramas.) Thirteen stages were seldom used, but Temple 16 at the Classic Maya site of Copán, Honduras, was so raised. The number refers to the 13 levels of heaven.

Another inference may come from the presently held idea that the room inside the temple was metaphorically understood as a cave. In all the Americas, ancient legends tell of the first humans emerging from caves. Actual caves were places of worship and initiation and were (are) thought to be the source of clouds and rain and the dwelling place of chthonic deities (or underworld energies). They are associated with engendering fertility and origins, as well as with death and underworld mysteries. The metaphoric potential of caves as signaled by these paradoxical associations—life and death, fertility and sterility—may indeed be evoked by the pyramid temple-cave placed skyward atop the "mountain." The use of dualities with paradoxical inversions to give potency to ideas and concepts is a profound trait in ancient Mesoamerican philosophies.

Water can be and was directly associated with the metaphors implicit in mountain and cave, but in Mesoamerica, little is known about how water was actually used in ceremony. In ancient Peru, the constructed channels within the great platforms of the Temple Complex of Chavín de Huántar leave little doubt about the use of water. In association with the stalactite-shaped Great Image placed within the so-called Old Temple, meaningful associations to caves and running (or dripping) water within a mountain are unavoidable. Although seldom so literally depicted, later pyramid platforms (the Akapana at Tiwanaku, Bolivia) and huacas (at Kenko, just outside of Cuzco, for example) continue to demonstrate the importance of water in ancient Peruvian religious ritual. The architecture in the Temple-Fortress of Sacsahuamán, built some 2000 years after the Temple Complex of Chavín de Huántar still expresses a close connection between mountain, water, and cave.

Water plays an important role in Egyptian and Cambodian pyramid designs, but its metaphoric or ideological meanings are not well studied at this time and have seldom, if ever, been linked to the idea of cave. The use of the moat at Angkor Wat has been likened to the primordial oceans that surround the world, but in the larger built complex of the areas in which Angkor Wat is a part, there were built two great "lakes" called *barays* and

At Borobodur, pilgrims ascended in clockwise fashion around five terraced levels, known as the World of Form, until they reached the three circular terraces at the top, the World of Formlessness. Lining the route are more than 1300 carved panels, such as the ones shown here, illustrating the life and legends of Buddha. Viewing these carved stories while ascending the World of Form is known in Buddhist practice as *pradaksiná*.

intricate systems of canals. The lakes and canals have been described in practical terms as functioning reservoirs and aqueducts, but lately, it is being considered that these water features were symbolically related to the temple-tower and its metaphoric representation of the central world-mountain.

The Egyptian pyramids were also associated with water rituals. Herodotus reports a local belief held at the time of his fifth-century-B.C. visit to Egypt that within the Great Pyramid of Giza was a lake of water. More substantially, we know water was important in the rituals and celebrations that focused on the pyramid, because boats are major items included in the burial goods, and especially because the Valley Temple was placed on the Nile or connected to it by a canal. An important approach to the pyramid complex would be by water

The Pyramid of the Niches, at El Tajín in Mexico, is part of a city that flourished from about A.D. 600 to 900. The niches that give the structure its name are said to number 365—one for each day in the year—but this figure has been disputed since, with deterioration over time, it is hard to know whether or not certain forms constitute niches.

to the Valley Temple, which was connected by the causeway to the Cult Temple (or Mortuary Temple) built against the eastern flank of the pyramid.

In their ideological function of affirming order, pyramids were also built to illustrate this order. Both the stupa and the Khmer temple-tower literally incorporated religious instruction into their designs and, thus, represented in a concrete way their ideological function. For both, the processional pathway was integrated into their plans by reflecting a mandala-like symmetry. Thus, the pilgrim walking the prescribed path physically experienced the great macrocosmic structure embedded in its microcosmic reflection and, at the same time, witnessed the beauty of narrative scenes carved to show him his way, indeed to explain the way through vividly wrought but well-known scenes. Around the processionals of the stupa, relief-carved scenes would portray the life and legends of Buddha, while the processionals of the Khmer temple-towers would illustrate scenes that sometimes mixed Buddhist images with more ancient Hindu myths.

The pyramid as a place of instruction, wherein ideologies are concretely expressed in plan, as well as illustrated with art works, may have been important for the designs of ancient Mesoamerican pyramids, especially those of the Maya and for the peoples who built the ancient city of El Tajín, in the state of Veracruz on the east coast of Mexico. Representational reliefs were carved on the lintels and wall panels of many Maya pyramid temples, and at El Tajín, carved wall panels were found in a ruined temple atop the Pyramid of the Niches. While it should be noted that these relief carvings are generally considered by scholars to be historical and political in content, these meanings do not preclude the possibility of religious instruction, and any representational imagery directly associated with a pyramid might well be explored for this more ideological function.

So far as I am aware, no contemporary texts—or any other archaeological evidence—exist to suggest that the ancient Sumerian ziggurat incorporated relief-carved displays of instructional imagery within its designs. And while it may be that part of the purposes associated with the relief carvings in the temple complexes built around the Egyptian pyramid were to instruct, this is difficult to argue. The images carved and painted within the temple complex associated with the pyramid more clearly illustrate ideals for a good life—hunting, eating, dancing, familial pleasures—and if an ideology is embedded as part of their meaning, then, superficially at least, it appears existentially materialistic. Such a characterization, however, may have little to do with the understandings of the ancient Egyptian pilgrim walking the passageway between the Valley Temple and the Cult Temple placed against the eastern side of the pyramid. Regardless of how we might understand the functions of the pyramid temple complexes, they are associated with the pyramid, but in no way are they integrated into its design. They are separated from the pyramid not only by the actuality of their placement, but also by their more human scale and by their horizontal orientation.

One can imagine, however, that all pyramids were intended to instruct or inspire people through their very forms, that they were aesthetic objects of contemplation and meditation, and that they were the embodiment of perfect order and ideal form. Interestingly enough, there is little evidence from which to deduce this as original intention. Commentators and critics of the Egyptian pyramid discuss its "pure" geometric form, but we do not know what the ancient builders thought about their pyramid's form. Students of Indian architecture speak of the stupa's embodiment of perfection as the body of Buddha, not because of its use of circle and square. The equation of symmetry and geometric abstraction with ideal perfection is from an ancient Greek aesthetic, and the Greeks did not build pyramids. The idea that the pyramid represents a perfect form may be a later addition to its list of functions rather than one with which it was originally endowed. That all pyramids were designed to make manifest universal or cosmic order is a closer description of their original ideological functions.

THE UNNECESSARY PROJECT

Another trait common to all pyramids is that there was never a compelling reason to build them in the first place. They did not provide shelter, nor were they used as places to store food, although a popular medieval European legend had them functioning as the biblical Joseph's granaries. Many ancient peoples flourished without building pyramids—the Greeks are a good example. If the pyramid was not originally built to assist in the biological or social survival of

The mobilization of huge numbers of laborers to build the Egyptian pyramids was a triumph not only of organization, but also of nation-building. This chalk relief from the tomb of Nefer-Seshem-Ptak, a ruler of the New Kingdom period, shows construction laborers under the direction of an overseer. Beginning with the construction of Zoser's Complex, at Saqqara in Lower Egypt, pyramid projects brought together workers from throughout Egypt, contributing to a sense of national endeavor.

its people, how do we account for the vast amounts of cultural and economic energy, time, and materials that went into their construction? As modern students (usually historians and archaeologists) looking back at ancient times and the developments that occurred and accrued to the present, we tend to look for the economic bottom line to explain how things happened and changes occurred, asserting that the economics of survival and power underlie human history and achievement, whether ancient or modern. This is referred to as "cultural ecology," and with its percepts, we try to offer a unified rationale for human behavior and history.

What necessity was the mother of the pyramid? Kurt Mendelssohn has proposed that the building of great pyramids, which had few material benefits accompanying their completion, occurred at certain specific times early in civilization's history. The pyramids were, according to Mendelssohn, the catalysts for the achievement of true statehood. Before the pyramids were built, ancient Egypt was a loose confederation of competing *nomes*, or tribes, ranging along the Nile, each with its own deity and governed by its own tribal nomarch (leader). The "pyramid project" required different and new communal strategies, calling for the talents of a civil service—the procurement and organization of large labor forces, stockpiling of building materials, and so forth—rather than those of the more dispersed priesthood and tribally insular families. Today, most scholars, including Mendelssohn, do not consider the pyramid work force to have been made up of coerced laborers or slaves. The majority of workers were unskilled and hired during the agricultural off-season. Their specialized (non-farming) tools and needs for food and water while working would have to be provided—someone had to "pay." Towns needed to be built to house the labor force and their families. More importantly, the bringing together of many different peoples from different tribes had the unifying effect of engendering a sense of nationality. As Mendelssohn writes:

> The pyramid project was creating a type of community which had never existed before. Tribal villagers were welded by common work into people with the consciousness of nationhood. It was probably for the first time that they thought of themselves first and foremost as Egyptians. Working together, under one administration, their differences and mutual suspicions were bound to lessen.

Mendelssohn points out that from the time of Zoser and the Third Dynasty pyramids were being built almost continuously throughout the Old Kingdom. The "pyramid project" began with clear desires for monumentality in the newly conceived stepped pyramid, built for Zoser by the architect Imhotep. The project reached its full potential during the reign of Sekhemket at the beginning of the Fourth Dynasty, continued with the creation of the magnificent pyramids at Giza, and ended in the Fourth Dynasty. Achieving the benefits of statehood are the supposed necessities behind the development and refinement of the ancient Egyptian pyramid during the Old Kingdom.

Mendelssohn goes on to consider another massive building project undertaken at a similar point in the social history of another civilization, that is, at the beginning of their statehood. The Pyramid of the Sun at Teotihuacán, he suggests, was built for the same reasons as those outlined for the Egyptian, although the people of Teotihuacán achieved statehood 3000 years later. Again, the pyramid project was a means of creating the popular unity and affection necessary for the successful political formation of statehood. And indeed, most anthropologists believe the city of Teotihuacán to have been the center of the first powerful state in Mesoamerica.

Archaeologist Bruce Dahlin picks up Mendelssohn's insights and extends them to the ancient Maya region. While Mendelssohn is unimpressed by most Mesoamerican pyramids, "the Aztec and Maya pyramids...are far inferior to the huge monuments of the Egyptian Pyramid Age proper," Dahlin argues that "We must conclude that the Maya were unconcerned, to a very great degree, with constructional and functional efficiency." He goes on to consider, "their most important function—the employment of large labor surpluses. What evidently was important to the Maya was the act of building these colossal structures, not the uses to which they would be put afterwards." This is precisely what Mendelssohn believes to be the meaning behind the Egyptian pyramid: "What mattered was not the pyramid—it was *building* the pyramid."

Mendelssohn's thesis, and Dahlin's application of it to explain the ancient Maya pyramid, is compelling in its elegant logic. And very likely, it is essentially correct to attribute a direct connection between the achievement of statehood and the economic efforts that were expended in the building of pyramids. Mendelssohn, however, goes further in his explanations by attributing to the ancient Egyptian builders an almost conscious desire for the benefits of statehood: that "employment of labour on an immense scale was the main political and economic object," and that this labour was employed in a project engendered by the "primitive urge" of making a distinctive mark, likened to "children making a sand castle." Mendelssohn's historical perspective is not that of an ancient Egyptian. He uses those ideas that modern Western statehood gave birth to—rather than the ideas that impelled statehood—such as cultural and spiritual energy being driven and inspired by economic and political concerns, as well as a vision of human history that parallels the biological development of the individual from birth and childhood to maturity, old age, and death. While an ancient Egyptian might wholeheartedly reject Mendelssohn's theory, this does not make his theses wrong, but they do have the advantages and disadvantages of an etic, or objective, point of view.

Although the very human desire for economic and political power surely played a major role in the building of any pyramid, there are other facets to human desire besides fulfilling the need for shelter, food, reproduction, and power, and these also make up part of the explanation for the "unnecessary" project of the pyramid. The need for social order is mirrored in a desire for a transcendent order of universal scope; the need for community is reflected in the human desire for identification with, and meaningful connection to, the universal, not just the particular and existential. Achieving the power to accumulate the material benefits of wealth or statehood and having access to the technical and material necessities for building a pyramid does not mean that someone will necessarily build a pyramid. More ephemeral, but very human, factors are just as necessary in causing a pyramid to rise.

The less pragmatic spiritual and aesthetic factors are easier to perceive when we look at how various pyramids were given form. To do this requires a combination of the emic and etic points of view. We have no choice but to look at the pyramid's form with our modern eyes and percepts, but we can consider the pyramid's form as a fit solution to an ancient problem. We can see the answer; now what was the question?

The role that pyramids played in the lives of the people who lived near them varied considerably. Mesoamerican pyramids provided dramatic Stairways led to their summits, and ceremonies could be held in and around these temples, as can be imagined from the powerful silhouette

MEMORIALS AND DRAMATIC STAGES

I n general, pyramids can be divided into two large and clearly different groups: the pyramid as memorial and the pyramid as a dramatic stage. The distinctions that determine classification into either memorial or stage are drawn from the ways humans interact with the architectural forms of the pyramids. The Egyptian pyramids of the Old Kingdom offer the best examples of the memorial function, while the ancient Mesoamerican pyramids are the best examples of dramatic stages. The Sumerian ziggurat

stages for religious rituals and civic ceremonies.
of El Castillo, at Chichén Itzá, Mexico.

surely was a dramatic stage, but few of these structures are left, and little is really known about them. It is likely that the early Buddhist stupas were conceived of as memorials, places that aroused contemplation, but the stupa of Borobodur, built in the eighth century with infusions of Hinduism and Chinese ideals, was designed as a most dramatic stage.

There is a distinct difference in time between the production of the ancient Mesoamerican and Egyptian pyramids—the Egyptian pyramids date to the third millennium B.C., and the Mesoamerican tradition begins, at the earliest, during the first millennium B.C.—but this difference is not necessarily a signal that the Egyptian pyramids should enjoy a more profound cultural position in the history of humankind. In fact, if primacy is important, then this belongs to the magnificent platforms and pyramids constructed during the fourth millennium B.C. along the coast and in the mountains of Peru.

There are several functional similarities between the Egyptian pyramids of the Old Kingdom and the pyramids of ancient Mesoamerica: they each present enormous human-made forms rising above contiguous features to mark a place with monumental significance; they each required tremendous expenditures of cultural, economic, and human energy to build; and in both traditions, the design of the pyramid reflected or represented the order of the universe as it was understood by its builders. In plan the pyramids are similar, both reflecting in their orientations the importance of the cardinal directions. It is in their vertical elevations that they differ: the stepped form of ancient Mesoamerica and the smooth, geometric form of ancient Egypt represent different visions of humankind's relationship to the heavens and to cosmic order. Furthermore, they differ in where they were built. The Egyptian pyramid was built in the desert well beyond towns and habitable land, while the Mesoamerican pyramid was a major feature of civic space. One was placed outside normal habitation, the other within, thus defining normal, daily experiences.

That the relationship between human beings and the heavens was a crucial issue at the time of death seems borne out by the fact that both Egyptian and Mesoamerican pyramids functioned as burials or cenotaphs. Until the middle of this century, however, the function of burial was always cited as a major difference between the two pyramid-building traditions: the pyramids of ancient Mesoamerica were thought to be simply a focus for religious ceremony and not to contain burials. After the great Mexican archaeologist, Alberto Ruz Lhuillier, discovered an extraordinary tomb in 1952, built beneath the Temple of Inscriptions at Palenque, archaeologists have come to expect that they will find burials located within most of the great pyramidal constructions found throughout Mesoamerica. (Actually, looters seem to have known that these pyramids functioned as burials long before the specialists.)

PYRAMIDS AS MEMORIALS

The famous pyramids of Egypt's Fourth Dynasty were built of limestone, a rock that can withstand the weatherings of time almost forever. (Limestone's "natural" enemy, carbon dioxide, has in recent years been joined by a new threat, carbon monoxide.) Some of the lesser pyramids of Egypt's Old Kingdom were deprived of their shapes and functions by the reuse of their already-cut limestone blocks, or because they were built of adobe, a friable material. But if the pyramid was truly monumental, such as those of Khufu, Chefren, and Menkaure at Giza, the human effort needed to "quarry" or reuse their multi-ton, limestone blocks would have been tremendous, and only the prized stone used for facing the pyramids was worth the taking. The pyramids themselves did not disappear and their original function as memorials remains intact.

The Giza pyramids were built with shaped blocks weighing between one and two tons each and laid without mortar. The manner in which the inner coursings were laid within the Giza pyramids, however, is not precisely known, but as discussed in Chapter 3, it is supposed that the inner coursings were not laid in continuous horizontal rows of blocks reflecting the square base, but as a series of concentric "frames" around a central core. Furthermore, each frame was laid with its coursings of stone angled downward from the outer edge of the frame toward the core of the pyramid. This structure would be the inner pyramid, the concentric frames creating a stepped pyramid as each "frame" corresponds to each rising step. The topmost step would be

Although the pyramids of Giza were elegantly finished with a fine, hard limestone quarried in Tura, on the east side of the Nile, most of this facing was stripped away over the centuries for use in other building sites. What we see today on the Pyramid of Chefren is the intermediate layer of regular limestone blocks, with just a small remnant of Tura limestone left intact at the very top.

the top of the central core, the trapezoidal nucleus around which the frames are laid. Essentially, the frames would compartmentalize and buttress the tremendous forces of weight and gravity, while their slanting, diagonal courses would stabilize and unify the integrity of the structure. As the weight of the total mass pushes down and out, it is counterbalanced by the frames with their angled courses leaning inward toward the core. The principle of this kind of construction is similar to that of the corbel, where two instabilities counterbalance each other to form a stable unit. The inner pyramid was constructed to last forever, and it has. For this is the pyramid, deprived of its finely cut outer stone casing, that we see today.

Finishing the pyramid was done with the famous Tura limestone cut from a quarry of the same name on the east side of the Nile and transported to the building site. The Tura limestone was harder than the local Giza stone, closer

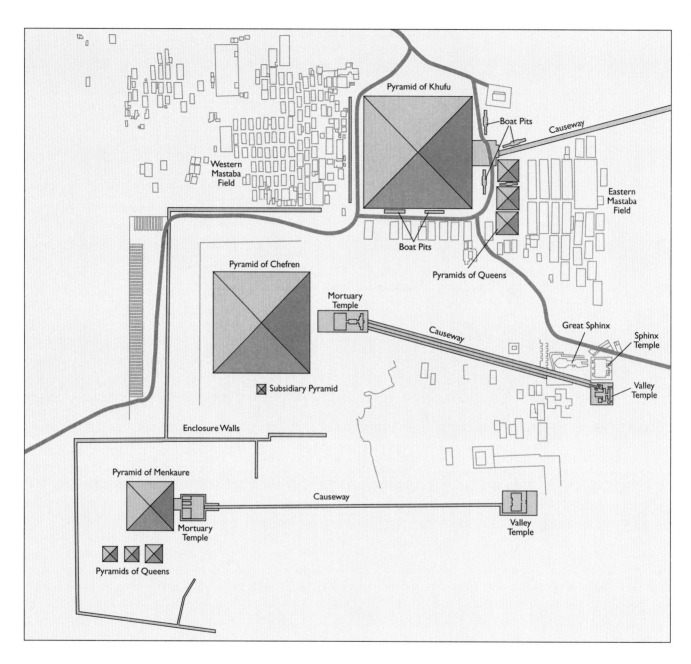

Western Mastaba Field

Pyramid of Khufu

Boat Pits

Causeway

Eastern Mastaba Field

Boat Pits

Pyramids of Queens

Pyramid of Chefren

Mortuary Temple

Causeway

Great Sphinx

Sphinx Temple

Valley Temple

☒ Subsidiary Pyramid

Enclosure Walls

Pyramid of Menkaure

Causeway

Mortuary Temple

Valley Temple

☒ ☒ ☒

Pyramids of Queens

The pyramids of Giza were each the focal point of shrines, temples and causeways, as illustrated above. The Valley Temple was the starting point for the procession that accompanied the dead pharaoh on the way to the Mortuary Temple.

in density to alabaster, thus making a protective, as well as aesthetically fine, surface. The blocks were carefully cut to the necessary irregular shapes, laid and fitted together with beautiful precision and, when in place, even more finely finished to achieve a smooth, crystalline surface. The internal passageways were closed by great barrier stones, and no vestige of openings to these inner spaces was visible from the outside.

The Giza silhouettes dominate the landscape, their pointed shadows reach out across the land, and their awesome mass and smooth surfaces seem grander than normal human comprehension. These monuments covering acres of land, these mountains, these "rays of the sun," were inviolable and closed. And yet, the pyramids of Giza were, and still are, the objects of pilgrimage. People travel long distances to view them and to stand in their presence—to feel and sense their imposing, age-old solemnity. The Giza pyramids were constructed by humankind for human purposes, and we instinctively feel that these purposes were grand and terrible ones.

The temples directly associated with the Egyptian pyramids are more accessible and informative, because the building scale is closer to human dimensions. Human participation takes place in the Valley and Cult temples and the covered causeway or path that connects them. It is in these places that relief-carved and painted images illustrate the giving of offerings, as well as various life activities—hunting, farming, cooking, feasting, and worshipping. And although the glyphs may cite the particular names of the deceased and his or her family, the illustrations seem to be about all lives, that is, they are generalized into recognizable events that could occur in any life. Seldom if ever in the Old Kingdom would unique events from one person's history or life be illustrated. Thus, if we are correct in our understanding of what the temple and causeway imagery means, its function, in large part, is to perpetuate "normal" life, in an abstract sense for the dead person, and in a concrete way by instructing the pilgrim who walks the course between the Valley Temple and the Cult Temple.

The simple but elegant contours of the pyramids at Giza stand as they have for millennia, enduring sentinels silhouetted against the sky. These artificial mountains, imposing in their age-old solemnity, remain objects of pilgrimage today. However, by their form, the pyramids of Egypt are closed and inaccessible to human penetration.

Other than regarding it as an overwhelming object of contemplation, the pilgrim does not interact with the pyramid itself. By its architectural design, the pyramid itself is inaccessible to human interaction. In its original state, it could not be scaled or penetrated. It is a closed form. Contrary to common assumptions, the Egyptian pyramid, closed and impenetrable to priest and pilgrim alike, is an almost unique conception when compared to all other traditions. The pyramids of Giza are neither the rule nor the gauge, but rather the exception.

PYRAMIDS AS DRAMATIC STAGES

The purpose in comparing ancient Egyptian and Mesoamerican pyramids is not to argue for primacy or for the greater validity of one tradition over the other, but to show by their comparison that the Mesoamerican tradition required human participation and interaction beyond the initial construction and beyond its initial function as marker and burial. If the Egyptian pyramid is a memorial for contemplation, the Mesoamerican pyramid is a dramatic stage for religious rituals and civic ceremonies. Its placement within the city, the building techniques used, and the formal changes that it undergoes throughout its active history, all point to its major function as a dramatic stage of cosmic design.

The impressive rise and sweep of the stairways, often framed by balustrades, and the commanding views offered by the high, terraced platforms, suggest that the pyramids were host to formal and dramatic events. Moreover, chronicles written during the Conquest and early colonial periods assure us that the pyramid platforms were indeed stages for ritual and public ceremony. Some pyramids, such as the Temple of Inscriptions at Palenque, have small stairways running up their sides or backs, allowing priests and actors access to the upper regions of the platforms without having to take the very public ascent up the main stairs—they could just appear. Humans walked up and down the stairs, ranged along the platforms, and appeared and disappeared into the small temples and back stairways. In a very authentic way, the Mesoamerican pyramid literally supported human action. And while the ceremonial dramas may have referred to events in the past—probably to historical and what we would call mythological times—they were nonetheless played out in the present.

The ancient Mesoamerican pyramid was never constructed to withstand all time. Its heartings were not designed with carefully engineered stone coursings, but were made instead of rubble-fill, mud-mortar, or adobe (sun-dried) bricks. The exteriors were finished with thin veneers of facing stones, more or less smoothly finished and set with generous amounts of mortar. The actual finishing of the exterior was accomplished with a wash of limestone stucco that would cover any irregularities in the facing stones. The stucco would be smoothed to a proper, probably aesthetically determined, surface and then painted. Nothing about the construction of the Mesoamerican pyramid bespeaks a desire on the part of the original builders to create a structure that would never fall apart. Clearly, they counted on continual maintenance and/or rebuilding projects, because the very materials they chose would require constant upkeep. In fact, the materials and construction techniques were not that different from those used for domestic architecture, then and now, and Mesoamerican homes, like ours, are in constant need of repair and upkeep.

It is instructive to note that the ancient Egyptians chose stone for the construction of pyramid-memorials and adobe for domestic architecture. Here

Its layers peeled away like those of an onion, the excavation of the Templo Mayor—the heart of the Aztec capital of Tenochtitlán—has revealed that the structure was rebuilt and expanded at least seven times. These reconstructions seem to have occurred with each generation, an interval that also corresponds with the 52-year cycle of the Aztec calendar. Shown in the foreground of this photo is part of the temple's western side, built around 1470, which featured an undulating stone-and-stucco serpent.

again, in the original conceptions exemplified by the Egyptian pyramid, a distinction—separation—from everyday human activity was important.

In the archaeological literature about ancient Mesoamerica, architectural structures are often described as "onions" because the requirements for continual maintenance and rebuilding just described are evident in the archaeological remains. As the archaeologist digs a trench into an ancient structure, the remains of the earlier constructional stages are discovered: the older facing stones and walls of earlier buildings found one after another—like the skins of an onion—as the intruding trench reveals the heartings of the pyramid.

Often the pyramid was "maintained" by constructing ever-larger versions over the existing form and plan. As mentioned earlier, a telling example of this is the Mexica, or Aztec, pyramid build at Tenayuca in the central Valley of Mexico. At least eight separate constructions have been detected within the body of the final pyramid, each one apparently like its earlier version, but now larger. All are defined by a plan that is essentially square in dimension and by an impressive elevation marked by a double stairway. Wide balustrades frame the stairs and "break" their angle of rise near the top to create imposing projections from the topmost platform on which two temples, reflecting the two stairways, were situated. The broken balustrades are dramatic forms. They not only create theatrical projections for the uppermost platform, they make the experience of walking up the stairs an impressive one, where the broken balustrades alternately hide and reveal the temples and whatever events were taking place on the top platform.

Built circa A.D. 1000 to 1200 at Chichén Itzá, in Mexico's Yucatán peninsula, El Castillo provides evidence for the theory that Mesoamericans ritually "buried" their temples. Excavations revealed an inner stairway that led to the discovery of a smaller pyramid inside the existing one. The earlier structure appeared to have been carefully preserved prior to being covered. The time difference between the two building phases—little more than a generation or two—suggests that the reconstruction of the pyramid may have been a regular undertaking.

PREVIOUS PAGE: **When the Aztecs founded their capital, Tenochtitlán, they immediately built a temple to honor their deity, Huitzilopochtli. This structure, known to us as the Templo Mayor, was the focal point around which the city grew. The temple was enlarged every 50 years or so by the addition of a new covering of stone, which was then sheathed in painted stucco. This illustration shows construction workers, under the direction of an architect, laying the facing stones for one of these periodic reconstructions.**

Even given the relative fragility of the materials used in the construction of the Tenayuca pyramid, its revealed history of rebuilding and enlargement is apparently redundant and seems not to have been strictly motivated by structural necessity alone. The number of rebuilding projects, approximately eight, and the supposed date of the original or first pyramid, which is approximately A.D. 1200, would require that every succeeding generation must have had to enlarge the structure in order to account for its rebuilding history, a process that we know came to an abrupt halt in A.D. 1519 with the arrival of the Spanish conquerors and their priests.

One theory about "unnecessary" rebuilding projects considers that the earlier pyramids were ritually buried—"pyramid burials". This is nicely illustrated by the famous pyramid at Chichén Itzá in the Yucatán, called El Castillo, or the castle. An earlier pyramid found within the newer construction seems to have been carefully preserved, including the temple with its stucco decorations, as well as what seems to be significant furniture. It is estimated that the time span between the construction of the earlier, smaller pyramid and the later one is no more than a generation or two. Given the short time difference and because the older pyramid and temple were found in good condition, it hardly seems possible that the newer construction was undertaken because the older one had become structurally degraded. Other reasons must be advanced to explain such rebuilding projects—of which "pyramid burial" is one—wherein ideological rather than material causes are important.

Other Mesoamerican pyramids have revealed different constructional histories in their successive plans and elevations. While displaying the expected history of rebuilding and reconstruction, the newer buildings can be quite different in plan or elevation from those they cover. Such differences suggest

Adorning the facade of the earlier Temple of Quetzalcóatl at Teotihuacán is a series of sculpted heads, both three-dimensional and bas-relief. Usually described as serpents, the sculptured heads are connected by the body of a feathered serpent that seems to undulate around seashells. In its original form, this dramatic sculptured work was stuccoed and brilliantly painted.

different in plan or elevation from those they cover. Such differences suggest that a remodeling or a revisioning of the meanings and functions of the original structure caused what we might call its modernization. Two good, but different, examples of remodeling can be illustrated by looking at the building histories of Teotihuacán's Temple of Quetzalcóatl, or the Feathered Serpent, and the Pyramid of the Magician at Uxmal in the northwest Yucatán.

The earlier version of the Temple of Quetzalcóatl is the most famous and, indeed, its exuberant sculpture gives the pyramid its name. The structure of the pyramid is formed by the two basic units, talud and tablero, for which Teotihuacán is famous, wherein the angled mass of the pyramid is defined by the talud and the stepped platforms are defined by the vertical and horizontal planes of the tablero. The Temple of Quetzalcóatl presents within its tableros tenoned heads usually described as serpents. These projecting heads are repeated units themselves and are graphically distinguished as geometrically composed heads alternating with organically formed heads. The two heads are connected by a feathered serpent body carved in low relief as if undulating around seashells. Originally, the whole affair was stuccoed and painted with beautiful and brilliant colors.

This early version of the Temple of Quetzalcóatl is an extraordinary architectural experience—monumental size, vivid color, complex surfaces with a rhythmic alternation of projecting heads joined by sinuous undulations in low relief, all composed within the formal, architectural tension between the vertical risings of the tableros and the slanted, angled rise of the taluds.

About the middle of the fifth century, the ancient Teotihuacános remodeled the Temple of Quetzalcóatl by covering up the exuberant surface of its principal facade with the more usual and definitely more austere forms of the unadorned talud and tablero. Clearly, this remodeling reflected quite a different idea on the part of the later builders as to how the pyramid's function and meaning should be given form.

The redesigning of the pyramid's surfaces seems to have happened at more or less the same time as the appearance of a particular warrior figure in the art of many ancient Mesoamerican cities. Most scholars agree that this figure represents a warrior because of its costume and the weapons it holds. It is more speculative, however, to consider the widespread image of the warrior as representing an interregional, or even an international, sodality whose ideals of austerity were likened to, or fashioned after, military rigor and discipline. Certainly, we know that two such militaristic sects or sodalities—the Jaguar Knights and the Eagle Knights—were in existence before and at the time of the Spanish Conquest. It may be conjecture, but it is possible that such a sodality or sect existed much earlier in the time of Teotihuacán and that it disapproved of the visual opulence represented in the early Temple of Quetzalcóatl. In its rebuilding, the temple is reformed: actually re-formed by covering up and, thus, eliminating the painted sculpture, and ideologically reformed by representing the now more desirable and abstracted austerities of the plain talud and tablero.

The Pyramid of the Magician has a different and, indeed, more complex rebuilding history that begins sometime in the seventh century A.D. In its first state, it was not a pyramid at all, but a range-type structure—a long, relatively low building whose interior spaces are seemingly as important as its exterior forms and often described as a palace. (While pyramids are constructed as solid mass and function as markers for burials and as dramatic platforms supporting small temples, palaces are constructed with walls that envelop interior voids or spaces and more closely resemble our ideas of architectural function as shelter.) In its first state, the "pyramid" at Uxmal faced to the west and, thus, inward toward the other buildings of the city.

It is in the second rebuilding phase that the structure becomes an actual pyramid, and so it remains throughout its building history. As defined by archaeological tunneling and estimation, the pyramid is enlarged, and its temple changes forms and decorations at least three more times. Even its orientation, that is, whether its temples faced to the east or to the west, seems to have changed. That the orientation should be toward the west is to be expected—the pyramid faced into the city—but when facing the east, the structure seemingly turned its back on the city to look outward. Both directions, east and west, are to be expected, but usually one pyramid expresses one direction.

The last remodeling of the Pyramid of the Magician took place around A.D. 1000 and seems to have been a synthetic "readout" of its own history. It is topped

The Pyramid of the Magician at Uxmal, Mexico, was originally a long, low building (possibly a palace). After its construction in the seventh century A.D., the structure was transformed into a pyramid, and underwent at least four subsequent rebuildings. The orientation of the pyramid changed more than once, sometimes facing away from the city center. The final construction phase took place around A.D. 1000, with the addition of another long structure atop the earlier temple, giving the pyramid its distinctive asymmetrical silhouette.

by a range-type structure that faces both east and west, while on its west face, a small temple—the so-called Chenes Temple—of the fourth rebuilding program is left exposed to be part of its new design, functioning as temple and as a pedestal for a new terrace or staging area constructed on what was once its roof. Viewed from the north or the south, the final version of the Pyramid of the Magician has a decidedly asymmetrical silhouette. It seems to lean or push to the west.

MEMORIAL AND STAGE: IDEOLOGICAL DIFFERENCES

When Kurt Mendelssohn and Bruce Dahlin consider the meaning of the pyramid as residing in its construction, they are thinking of the pyramid as representing a solution for social enterprises bound for national or at least civic unity, and they both accept the achievements of the Egyptian builders as the more perfect embodiment of such an effort. But the fact is the ancient Mesoamerican builders had access to permanent materials—limestone, basalt, and volcanic stones—and they chose not to use them. In this final section, it is assumed that the designs rendered by ancient Mesoamerican architects were right to begin with; that they were the correct solutions to fulfill perceived needs, and were not in any way compromised by lack of vision or ability.

Several important differences between the ancient Mesoamerican and the Egyptian pyramid have been cited. These differences are: (1) the methods of construction, known through archaeological investigation, (2) the construction materials, and (3) the elevations of the original designs. The Egyptian pyramids were built as a single, one-time project with materials chosen for their permanence. Their design is an abstract, geometric shape physically inaccessible to human interaction. Each Mesoamerican pyramid was rebuilt and/or redesigned many times throughout its active history. It was built with materials that required maintenance and upkeep, and it was designed as a rising series of stepped platforms to dramatically support and enhance human actions. A key difference between the two traditions has to do with the way the pyramids were conceived and designed in relationship to living people.

These differences may tell us how the ancient builders thought about their pyramids—what may have been some of the conceptual ideals behind their design and function. The ziggurats of Sumeria are similar to the Mesoamerican pyramid because of their stepped or staged elevations, and archaeology demonstrates that they too went through histories of extensive rebuilding programs. The early Buddhist stupas may have been conceived along the outlines drawn here for the Egyptian pyramids. Not enough archaeological information is available for the Khmer temple-towers or the Chinese burial tumuli to draw any close analogies.

One of the most intriguing ideas has to do with the necessity of human action and interaction required by the Mesoamerican pyramid. They needed constant maintenance by successive generations in order to remain structurally viable. In some cases, archaeological evidence shows that the various rebuildings and remodelings took place through time in a generational rhythm, and were undertaken more for ceremonial or ritual reasons rather than practical necessity. Either way, the original architects counted on their pyramid's receiving continued human investment and devotion.

The Mesoamerican pyramid was, in effect, under constant care and construction; it therefore functioned as a place of daily activity, and was not simply a closed memorial to a past event. Furthermore, the ancient Mesoamerican pyramid served as a stage for dramatic public ceremonies. Celebrations, such as those honoring anniversaries, may have referred to events of the past, but they took place in the present.

Such observations may seem simple, but lead to rather intriguing and logical insights. That people were required to participate continually in defining a pyramid reveals a profound belief that human participation was necessary for the maintenance of the universe. Such a requirement is very similar to the creation story told in the *Popol Vuh*, a narrative of the highland Maya peoples, the Quiché. This relates the gods' abortive efforts to create human beings before humankind as we know it was finally achieved. The earlier beings had been rejected by the gods because they all failed in one important criterion: that they should be able to speak in order to praise the gods, to remember them, and to keep their days, for if something is forgotten, truly out of mind and out of memory, it ceases to exist. Here the Quiché gods know that if they are forgotten, if their days are not kept, then they cease to be. They need humans. They need a continual interaction with human beings. This story is based on the same profound expectation of continuing human participation that I have described for the pyramids.

Mesoamerican pyramids served as a stage for dramatic public ceremonies. Bloodletting was ritually carried out in public view, as was the excision of hearts, both human and animal.

The necessity for human participation in the maintenance of the cosmos and for the actions of the gods is the reason usually given to explain the ancient Mesoamerican tradition of sacrifice and bloody penances. The ancient legends also say that at the beginning of time, the gods sacrificed themselves in order to set up the cosmic system and to get it moving in the first place so that human life could flourish. In return, humans must sustain the gods and the cosmos by remembering, by repaying, thus continuing the initial sacrificial acts.

This belief in an active reciprocity between gods and humankind for the continuing creation of existence affords more than an explanation or an excuse for bloody sacrificial deeds. It is an insight into the ancient Mesoamerican philosophy wherein humans were necessary co-creators of the universe and co-designers of its order. The archaeological evidence suggests that this design, if exemplified by the pyramid, was, in part, actively redefined from one generation to the next.

Such a characterization for a necessary interaction between human and universe may be too particular for the ancient ziggurat and its perceived purposes. However, few would deny that the ziggurat functioned as a stage for religious ceremony and drama, or that its design was engendered by an ancient assumption about human participation in these activities. Finally, it is widely accepted that the materials used in the ziggurat's construction would require continuing human commitment.

The Egyptian pyramid was conceived as a monumental memorial that would withstand all time regardless of the vagaries of man or nature. Human participation with its completed form was, and is, passive and contemplative. The energies of its builders focused on its established, eternal, and unchanging form. The ancient Mesoamerican pyramid was, in a fairly real sense, always in the process of being built. The focus of energies was on the processes of making and forming, not so much in the achievement of a final and stable form.

If the Mesoamerican pyramid was a dramatic stage, a place for human participation in the designs of the universe, a place where the cosmos and the human condition came together to be defined and redefined, then it is a remarkably fit symbol for the Americas. Its forms and ideologies come closer to supporting the needs of the world as it enters the 21st century than the symbol that stands for timeless perfection achieved by the social strategies of work and progress. It seems impossible that the Egyptian pyramids will ever lose their hold on humankind's imagination, for they are unique in their monumental and geometrically perfect forms, closed and impervious to time. They are the monuments of the past. The American pyramids, by their accessibility and changing forms, still offer themselves to the future.

POSTSCRIPT

In thinking about the American pyramid as a symbol still active in the present and a negotiable form for the future, I found myself rereading the 1972 essay, *The Other Mexico: Critique of the Pyramid*, by Octavio Paz, the great poet and statesman. "The other Mexico" refers to those Mexican people who are politically disenfranchised and live in terrible poverty and to an unconscious and ancient actuality that exists within all Mexicans. For this latter, Paz uses the phrase "an other Mexico," rather than "the other Mexico." Paz evokes the pyramid as a symbol for this unconscious reality of the Mexican people and is careful to point out that, despite its shadowy existence, the unconscious reality is an actuality, a fact of Mexican life, not a Jungian myth. He argues that what erupted on October 2, 1968—the day of the fateful massacre by government forces of students gathered together for peaceful protest in the plaza of Tlatelolco in Mexico City—was a manifestation of this actuality readily symbolized by the truncated pyramid. How does this explain the violence of that October day?

It is not clear whether Paz's complex essay argues against an implicit unfairness wherein those who are controlled must also provide the means for control—that is, their support—or whether Paz positively acknowledges that, despite its implicit inequities, such an interdependence between ruler and ruled allows people, individually or collectively, to choose how they will participate or act because interdependence insures their choice will have an effect.

The foundation of Mexico City's Plaza of the Three Cultures, pictured below, is the remains of the pyramid of Tlatelolco, the main ritual structure of the former commercial hub of the Aztec empire. The pyramid was razed by the Spanish following the fall of Tenochtitlán, Tlatelolco's larger twin, and a Roman Catholic church was constructed on the site. The pyramid is a fitting symbol for the downtrodden "other Mexico," as described by Octavio Paz.

And why is the pyramid an apt symbol for an other Mexico that runs in the hearts of all its people? Paz compares the geography of Mexico to the form of a pyramid. From its east and west coasts and from its northern and southern borders, it rises up its mountain chains to the apex of the central valley where Mexico City rests atop the older Mexica city of Tenochtitlán. The truncated top of the pyramid is the place where the four cardinal directions come together, where time begins and ends, and where the rituals of interdependence (between humans and gods; between humans and their society) are enacted that ultimately inspire terrible and bloody sacrifice.

Paz asks the Mexican people to face the reality of this "pyramid" within themselves, to critique it, and in so doing, to dissolve it, to extirpate its potency and threat to sanity. The sacrifices made on that day, October 2, 1968, in the plaza of Tlatelolco were, and still are, so great that any explanation seems ineffective. As I reread Octavio Paz's essay, I knew that my initial understanding of it had changed, although one insight had not: *The Other Mexico* is a cry of despair.

The truncated pyramid is the symbolic cause for Mexican desperation. But somehow, although Paz never says so, the descriptive qualifier, truncated, used throughout his text suggests an imperfect form. What I have tried to illustrate in this book is that geometric perfection for a pyramid finishes it. It can take no other form except to crumble, fall apart, and disappear. If we or future critics of pyramids were to rebuild the Egyptian pyramids, we would have to rebuild them as they had been; we would never reshape them, as nothing but their already perfect form would be acceptable. If we were to rebuild the pyramids of Mesoamerica (as has actually been done in many cases), there would be arguments about the "authenticity" of the reconstructed parts, but, in reality, our building would only continue what had been started so long ago. Disassembling the pyramid would deprive all of us of an essential, long abiding, and very human symbol, one not peculiar to the Mexican peoples. I suggest, instead, that because the truncated pyramid allows us to ascend to its top, we do so; we accept its formal invitation to critique and redefine its meanings. It is not a finished form; it is not closed to us.

REFERENCES

GENERAL

The references that follow include the standard works written about pyramids as well as works specifically cited throughout the text of this book. The literature on pyramids is extensive and ever-increasing. Two good sources for "keeping up" are the popular periodicals *National Geographic* and *Scientific American*.

CLAYTON, PETER A. AND MARTIN J. PRICE 1988 *The Seven Wonders of the Ancient World*. Routledge, London.

COE, MICHAEL 1957 Khmer Settlement Pattern: A Possible Analogy with That of the Maya. In *American Antiquity* 22:409-10.

COLVIN, HOWARD 1991 *Architecture and the After-Life*. Yale University Press, New Haven.

FRANKFORT, HENRI, MRS. H.A. FRANKFORT, JOHN A. WILSON, AND THORKILD JACOBSEN 1946 *The Intellectual Adventure of Ancient Man*. University of Chicago Press, Chicago.

PAZ, OCTAVIO 1972 *The Other Mexico: Critique of the Pyramid*. Lysander Kemp, trans. Grove Press, Inc., New York.

POPE, MAURICE 1975 *The Story of Archaeological Decipherment*. Charles Scribner's Sons, New York.

SCULLY, VINCENT 1979 *The Earth, the Temple, and the Gods*. Yale University Press, New Haven.

SEMENZATO, CAMILLO 1975 *The World of Art*. MacDonald General Books, London.

SPRAGUE DE CAMP, L. 1974 *The Ancient Engineers*. Ballantine Books, New York.

WILLEY, GORDON R. AND JEREMY A. SABLOFF 1980 *A History of American Archaeology* (2nd edition). Thames and Hudson, Ltd., London.

AMERICAN

ANDREWS, GEORGE F. 1975 *Maya Cities: Placemaking and Urbanization*. University of Oklahoma Press, Norman.

AVENI, ANTHONY 1980 *Skywatchers of Ancient Mexico*. University of Texas Press, Austin.

BERRIN, KATHLEEN AND ESTHER PASZTORY 1993 *Teotihuacán. Art from the City of the Gods*. The Fine Arts Museum of San Francisco and Thames and Hudson Ltd., New York.

BOONE, ELIZABETH HILL (EDITOR) 1987 *The Aztec Templo Mayor*. Dumbarton Oaks Research Library and Collection, Washington, D.C.

CHARNAY, DÉSIRÉ 1887 *The Ancient Cities of the New World*. Harper and Brothers, New York.

CIEZA DE LEÓN, PEDRO DE 1959 *The Incas of Pedro de Cieza de León*. Harriet de Onis, trans., Victor W. von Hagen, ed. University of Oklahoma Press, Norman.

DAHLIN, BRUCE 1981 *An Anthropologist Looks at the Pyramids: A Late Classical Revitalization Movement at Tikal, Guatemala*. Ph.D. Dissertation (1976), Temple University. University Microfilms International, Ann Arbor.

DONNAN, CHRISTOPHER B. (EDITOR) 1985 *Early Ceremonial Architecture in the Andes*. Dumbarton Oaks Research Library and Collection, Washington, D.C.

DÍAZ DEL CASTILLO, BERNAL 1956 *The Discovery and Conquest of Mexico*. A.P. Maudslay, trans. Noonday Press (Farrar, Straus and Giroux), New York.

EDMONSON, MUNRO (TRANSLATOR AND ANNOTATER) 1986 *Heaven Born Merida and Its Destiny. The Book of Chilam Balam of Chumayel*. University of Texas Press, Austin.

GARCILASO DE LA VEGA, INCA 1987 *Royal Commentaries of the Incas and General History of Peru* [1609]. H.V. Livermore, trans. University of Texas Press, Austin.

HARTUNG, HORST 1971 *Die Zeremonialzentren der Maya*. Akademische Druck-u. Verlagsanstalt, Graz, Austria.

HEIZER, ROBERT F., PHILIP DRUCKER, AND JOHN A. GRAHAM 1968 Investigations at La Venta, 1967. In *Contributions of the University of the University of California Archaeological Facility* 5:1-34. University of California, Department of Anthropology, Berkeley.

HEMMING, JOHN AND EDWARD RANNEY 1982 *Monuments of the Incas*. University of New Mexico Press, Albuquerque.

KUBLER, GEORGE 1984 *The Art and Architecture of Ancient America* (3rd [integrated] edition). The Pelican History of Art. Penguin Books, Baltimore.

LOPEZ AUSTIN, ALFREDO, LEONARDO LOPEZ LUJAN, AND SABURO SUGIYAMA 1991 The Temple of Quetzalcóatl at Teotihuacán. In *Ancient America* 2 (1):93-105.

MILLON, RENÉ, BRUCE DREWITT, AND JAMES A. BENNYHOFF 1965 The Pyramid of the Sun at Teotihuacán: 1959 Investigations. In *Transactions of the American Philosophical Society* No. 55, part 6. Philadelphia.

MOLINA-MONTES, AUGUSTO 1982 Archaeological Buildings: Restoration or Misrepresentation. In *Falsifications and Misreconstructions of Pre-Columbian Art*. Elizabeth H. Boone, ed., pp. 125-141. Dumbarton Oaks, Washington, D.C.

MOSELEY, MICHAEL E. 1975 *The Maritime Foundations of Andean Civilization*. Cummings Publishing Company, Menlo Park, California.

1992 *The Inca and Their Ancestors*. Thames and Hudson Ltd., London and New York.

RICKETSON, JR., OLIVER AND EDITH BAYLES RICKETSON 1937 *Uaxactún, Guatemala: Group E—1926-1931* Excavations and Artifacts. Carnegie Publication 477. Carnegie Institution of Washington, Washington D.C.

ROBERTSON, DONALD 1963 *Pre-Columbian Architecture*. The Great Ages of World Architecture. George Braziller, New York.

ROYS, RALPH 1933 *The Book of the Chilam Balam of Chumayel*. Publication 438, Carnegie Institution of Washington, Washington, D.C.

RUZ LHUILLER, ALBERTO 1973 *El Templo de las Inscripçiones Palenque*. Coleccion Cientifica 7, Instituto Nacional de Antropologia e Historia, Mexico D.F.

SMITH, ROBERT ELIOT 1987 A Ceramic Sequence from the Pyramid of the Sun, Teotihuacán, Mexico. In *Papers of the Peabody Museum of Archaeology and Ethnology 75*. Harvard University, Cambridge.

TEDLOCK, DENNIS 1985 *Popol Vuh. Translation and Commentary*. Simon and Schuster, New York.

Tenayuca: Official Guide (English). Instituto Nacional de Antropologia e Historia, Mexico D.F.

THOMPSON, J. ERIC S. 1970 *Maya History and Religion*. University of Oklahoma Press, Norman.

1974 Maya Astronomy. In *Philosophical Transactions of the Royal Society* 276:83-98. London.

TOMPKINS, PETER 1976 *Mysteries of the Mexican Pyramids*. Harper and Row, Publishers, New York.

TOWNSEND, RICHARD F. 1982 Pyramid and Sacred Mountain. In *Ethnoastronomy and Archaeoastronomy in the American Tropics*, Anthony Aveni and Gary Urton, eds., pp. 37-62. Annals of the New York Academy of Sciences No. 385. The New York Academy of Sciences, New York.

EGYPTIAN AND AFRICAN

BREASTED, JAMES HENRY 1912 *The Development of Religion and Thought in Ancient Egypt*. Charles Scribner's Sons, New York.

COTTRELL, LEONARD 1956 *The Mountains of Pharaoh*. Rinehart and Company, New York.

DAVID, A. ROSALIE 1986 *The Pyramid Builders of Ancient Egypt. A Modern Investigation of Pharaoh's Workforce*. Routledge and Kegan Paul, London.

EDWARDS, I.E.S. 1985 *The Pyramids of Egypt* (revised and updated). The Pelican History of Art. Penguin Books, Baltimore.

FAKHRY, AHMED 1969 *The Pyramids* (2nd edition). University of Chicago Press, Chicago.

GONEIM, M. ZAKARIA 1956 *The Buried Pyramid*. Longman, Green, and Co., London.

HAWASS, ZAHI A. 1990 *The Pyramids of Ancient Egypt*. Carnegie Museum of Natural History, Pittsburgh.

LAUER, J.P. 1957 Rebuilding Imhotep's Masterpiece. In *Archaeology* 10: 274-79.

LEMESURIER, PETER 1977 *The Great Pyramid Decoded*. St. Martin's Press, New York.

MENDELSSOHN, KURT 1974 *The Riddle of the Pyramids*. Thames and Hudson Ltd., London and New York.

SMITH, W.S. AND W.K. SIMPSON 1981 *The Art and Architecture of Ancient Egypt* (revised with additions). Pelican History of Art, Penguin Books, Baltimore.

SPENCER LEWIS, H. 1936 *The Symbolic Prophecy of the Great Pyramid*. Rosicrucian Library, Vol. XIV. Supreme Grand Lodge of AMORC, San Jose, California.

STEWART, DESMOND 1971 *The Pyramids and Sphinx*. Wonders of Man (series). Newsweek, New York.

TOMPKINS, PETER 1971 *Secrets of the Great Pyramid*. Harper and Row, New York.

NEAR EAST

CRAWFORD, HARRIET 1991 *Sumer and the Sumerians.* Cambridge University Press, Cambridge and New York.

LAMPL, PAUL 1968 *Cities and Planning in the Ancient Near East.* George Braziller, New York.

LLOYD, SETON 1978 *The Archaeology of Mesopotamia.* Thames and Hudson Ltd., London.

FRANKFORT, HENRI 1969 *The Art and Architecture of the Anceint Orient* (4th revised edition with additional bibliography). The Pelican History of Art, Penguin Books, Baltimore.

MALLOWAN, MAX E.L. 1965 *Early Mesopotamia and Iran.* McGraw-Hill, New York.

MASON, HERBERT 1972 *Gilgamesh. A Verse Narrative.* A Mentor Book from New American Library, New York.

MELLAART, JAMES 1965 *Earliest Civilizations of the Near East.* McGraw-Hill, New York.

MOORTGAT, ANTON 1969 *The Art of Ancient Mesopotamia.* Phaidon Publishers, London and New York.

PARROT, ANDRÉ 1955 *The Tower of Babel.* Edwin Hudson, trans.. Studies in Biblical Archaeology 2. Philosophical Library, New York.

1961 *Sumer. The Dawn of Art.* Stuart Gilbert and James Emmons, trans. Golden Press, New York.

STROMMENGER, EVA 1964 *Art of Mesopotamia.* Harry N. Abrams, Inc., New York.

WOOLLEY, SIR LEONARD 1939 *Ur Excavations, Vol. 5: The Ziggurat and Its Surroundings.* London and Philadelphia.

ASIAN

COEDES, GEORGE 1963 *Angkor. An Introduction* Emily F. Gardiner, trans. Oxford University Press, London.

FUJIOKA, MICHIO 1972 *Angkor Wat.* This Beautiful World No. 29. Kodansha International, Ltd., Tokyo.

FREEMAN, MICHAEL AND ROGER WARNER 1990 *Angkor. The Hidden Glories.* Houghton Mifflin Company, Boston.

GOVINDA, ANAGARIKA 1940 *Some Aspects of Stupa Symbolism.* Kitabistan, Allahabad and London.

GROSLIER, BERNARD AND JACQUES ARTHAUD 1966 *Angkor. Art and Civilization.* Frederick A. Praeger, Publishers, New York.

LI, HSUEH-CHIN 1985 *Eastern Zhou and Qin Civilizations.* Yale University Press, New Haven.

MAZZATENTA, O. LOUIS 1992 A Chinese Emperor's Army for Eternity, in *National Geographic,* Vol. 182(2): 114-130.

MYRDAL, JAN AND GUN KESSLE 1970 *Angkor. An Essay on Art and Imperialism.* Paul B. Austin, trans. Pantheon Books, New York.

ROWLAND, BENJAMIN 1970 *The Art and Architecture of India. Buddhist, Hindu, Jain.* The Pelican History of Art. Penguin Books, Baltimore.

STEINHARDT, NANCY SHATZMAN 1984 *Chinese Traditional Architecture.* China Institute in America, China House Gallery, New York.

SULLIVAN, MICHAEL 1984 *The Arts of China* (third edition). University of California Press, Berkeley.

THORP, ROBERT L. 1983 An Archaeological Reconstruction of the Lishan Necropolis. In *The Great Bronze Age of China,* George Kuwayama, ed., pp. 72-83. Los Angeles County Museum of Art, Los Angeles.

WU, HUNG 1988 From Temple to Tomb: Ancient Chinese Art and Religion in Tradition. In *Early China* 13:78-115.

WU, NELSON 1963 *Chinese and Indian Architecture.* The Great Ages of World Architecture, George Braziller, New York.

ZIMMER, HEINRICH 1955 *The Art of India Asia.* 2 volumes. Bollingen Series XXXIX, Pantheon Books, Inc., New York.

INDEX

PICTURE CREDITS

Front cover photograph by Dick Durrance II/Woodfin Camp & Associates.
Back cover photograph by Wolfgang Kaehler.

159

AUTHOR'S ACKNOWLEDGMENTS

Is it wonder that leads to knowledge or does knowledge lead to wonderment? Studying the world's pyramids provides excellent proof that both cases are true and inseparable. I hope I have engaged the reader's sense of wonder as well as presented information that might lead to some knowledge. I found surprising rewards in doing this project—small and large ones, some represented in the text, some not. For this I am deeply grateful to Jeremy Sabloff for asking me to join the Smithsonian series, *Exploring the Ancient World.*

The staff at St. Remy Press are definitely congenial. Chris Jackson and Geneviève Monette took on the onus of procuring illustrations; Philippe Arnoldi designed the book to emphasize both its overt and its more subtle contents, and Alfred LeMaitre patiently and intelligently guided me through all the matters of editing.

Robert Dash of Willamette University in Salem, Oregon, encouraged and supported my early efforts at understanding the differences between pyramid forms. Louise Maffitt was more than a sounding board for my thoughts and ideas about pyramids; this book owes a great deal to our wonderful conversations in which it was never clear who finished the sentences. Finally, it is to Joe Rothrock and to the standards of his generous intelligence that my greatest thanks and appreciation are given.

Flora S. Clancy
Albuquerque, New Mexico